## GCSE RELIGIOUS STUDIES for AQA

# ST. MARK'S GOSPEL

D1427456

**Gordon Geddes**
**Jane Griffiths**

**Heinemann**

Heinemann Educational Publishers
Halley Court, Jordan Hill, Oxford OX2 8EJ
Part of Harcourt Education

Heinemann is the registered trademark of
Harcourt Education Limited

Text © Gordon Geddes and Jane Griffiths, 2001

First published in 2001

07
10 9

**British Library Cataloguing in Publication Data**
A catalogue record for this book is available from the
British Library

ISBN:978-0-435306-94-6

Picture research by Jennifer Johnson
Designed and typeset by Artistix
Illustrations by Andrew Skilleter
Printed and bound in China by CTPS

**Acknowledgements**
The publishers would like to thank the following for
permission to reproduce copyright material:
pp. 82-3, HarperCollins for *Something Beautiful for
God* by Malcolm Muggeridge; p. 103, the Methodist
Service Book; p. 41, Polydor International, taken
from the booklet accompanying CD Archiv
Production BWV 244 English translation © 1984
Polydor International GmbH, Hamburg.

Cover photograph by AKG London

The publishers would like to thank the following for
permission to use photographs: Ancient Art and
Architecture Collection/Mary Jelliffe, p. 54; Andes
Press Agency/Carlos Reyes Manzo, pp. 4, 23, 33,
37, 61, 63, 71, 77, 80, 83, 87, 97, 99, 101, 102,
103, 105 and 113; Andes Press Agency/Val Baker,
p. 78; The Bridgeman Art Library, pp. 12, 39 and
95; Camera Press/Vanya Kewley, p. 57; Circa Photo
Library, pp. 68 and 101; Circa Photo Library/Barrie
Searle, p. 97; Circa Photo Library/John Fryer, pp. 23,
32 and 33; Corrymeela, p. 85; Covenant Players,
p. 77; Empics/Neal Simpson, p. 93; Format/Melanie
Friend, p. 74; Format/Sheila Gray, p. 84; Fortean
Picture Library, p. 67; Kevin Mayhew Ltd, p. 109;
Panos Pictures/Bruce Paton, p. 83; Panos
Pictures/Rhodri Jones, p. 49; Panos Pictures/Sean
Sprague, p. 80; Panos Pictures/Trygve Bølstad,
p. 72; Performing Arts Library/Clive Barda, p. 35; Zev
Radovan, pp. 11, 21, 29, 31 and 88; Scottish
National Gallery of Modern Art, p. 27; Graham
Snape, pp. 14, 59, 108, 110 and 111; Sonia
Halliday Photographs, pp. 23, 25, 40 and 43; Sonia
Halliday Photographs/David Silverman, p. 8; Sonia
Halliday Photographs/F. H. C. Birch, p. 69; Sonia
Halliday/Gabriel Loire, p. 80; Sonia Halliday
Photographs/Jane Taylor, p. 18; Sonia Hallliday
Photographs/Laura Lushington, p. 23 and 106.

The publishers have made every effort to contact
copyright holders. However, if any material has been
incorrectly acknowledged, the publishers would be
pleased to correct this at the earliest opportunity.

Tel: 01865 888058 www.heinemann.co.uk

# Contents

Welcome! We hope this book will be a useful resource in teaching GCSE students.

## What this book contains

This book is designed to support AQA's GCSE option of specification A for Religious Studies – The Christian Life and St Mark's Gospel.

The book is divided into sections, which provide full coverage of the specification. In each section there are a series of self-contained units. The units contain illustrations and key points which summarize the main learning points. At the end of each section there are exam hints and practice. Support for coursework is provided on pages 116–19.

Key terms taken from the specification are explained when first they appear. Other difficult words and phrases are found in the glossary and are in bold the first time they appear in a section.

### The New International Version

Passages from the Gospel are taken from the NIV. All set passages from the Gospel are given in full, with commentary. As all the passages are given in full, there is no need to have class sets of the Gospel.

## How best to use this book

As far as possible we follow the order of topics as printed in the specification. Teachers will decide for themselves whether this is the order in which they should teach the specification.

## Activities

Activities are given for each unit. They are mainly discussion or individual research topics. The activities are designed to develop knowledge and understanding of the specification content. They can also be used to develop Key Skills and are coded to show which Key Skill they might develop.

Some activities make use of Drama techniques:

- **Thought-tracking:** working in pairs or threes, pupils reconstruct an event. They use a handclap signal to indicate the change from speech to thought and back again. Others in the group can reply to speech but not to thought.

- **Hot seat:** the teacher or a student in role sits in the hot seat and has questions asked of them relating to their character. This can be used as exploration (with the teacher in role providing facts as answers), as revision (same format) when the questions become more important than the answers or, with a pupil in role helping to organize thought.

- **Forum theatre:** a scene is enacted, watched by the rest of the group, who can intervene to freeze the action, ask for clarification, add thought, take over a character or add another.

These techniques are well known to teachers of Drama; some Religious Education teachers may wish to consult Drama colleagues on the use of them.

We have been careful to cover assessment objectives AO1, AO2 and AO3. However, in the coursework section we have not used these terms with students but have made the ideas more accessible by referring to knowledge, understanding and evaluation.

Welcome! We hope you find this book helpful in your studies.

## About your AQA course

This book is designed to support AQA's GCSE option of specification A for Religious Studies – The Christian Life and St Mark's Gospel. If you are following a full course, the material in this book covers half the requirements of your GCSE. If you are following a short course, it covers all your needs.

You will be assessed in two ways. You will have to do coursework (for up to 20% of the marks for the short course and 10% for the full course). You will also have to do a written examination at the end of the course (for up to 80% of the short course marks and 40% of the full course).

## About this book

This book is divided into sections, which provide full coverage of all the topics in the specification. All set passages from the Gospel are given in full, with commentary. In each section there are a series of self-contained units. In each unit you will find illustrations and key points to summarize what you have learnt. At the end of each section there are exam hints and practice. On pages 116–19, support for your coursework is provided.

Key terms taken from the specification are explained when first they appear. Other difficult words and phrases are found in the glossary and are bold the first time they appear in a section.

## Hints on exam success

Remember that sound knowledge is the key to success in your GCSE. In particular, you must know the contents of the Gospel accurately and in detail.

Bible references are given in this way:
Mark chapter 1 verse 6: (1: 6)
Mark chapter 3 verses 1 to 6: (3: 1-6)

Note that in exam papers different Christian groups – e.g., Methodists, Roman Catholics, Baptists – may be called *either* traditions *or* denominations.

It is important that you understand that there are two different ways of marking exam questions.

- Some questions are marked point by point with a mark for each point made. Sometimes two marks may be given for a well-made point or one for a point which is clumsy or incomplete.
- Other questions are marked on levels of response. The examiner assesses the answer as a whole and decides at what level credit should be given.

Look at the following examples:

**Question:** What did Jesus say as he gave the bread and wine to his disciples at the Last Supper? (3 marks)

**Mark Scheme:** You would get one mark each for 'This is my body' and 'This is my blood'. As long as the terms body and blood are correctly used, phrases such as 'Here is my body' would be counted as correct. The third mark would be given for any further point, e.g., 'of the New Covenant'.

**Question:** Why do some Christians practise believers' baptism? (4 marks)

**Mark scheme:** To gain marks here you need to make clear that the persons being baptized should be able to understand the meaning of what they are doing. In the light of their understanding they should make a personal decision to commit themselves to following and serving Jesus as their Saviour. They are dying to sin and rising again to new life.

This is how an examiner would award marks for this question:

**Level 1:** An answer at this level would only contain one or two relevant basic points.
**Level 2:** An answer at this level would show some understanding of the meaning of the rite, at a simple level.
**Level 3:** At this level the student will have shown awareness not only of the need for understanding but also of the need for choice and/or commitment.
**Level 4:** To gain full marks the answer will need to cover convincingly most, though not necessarily all, the points above.

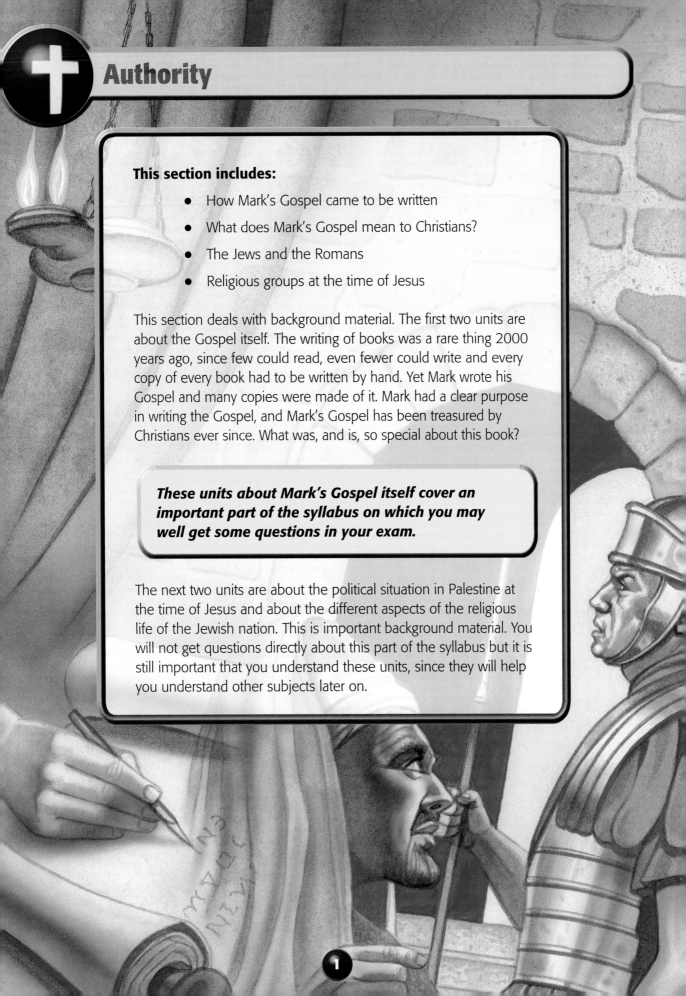

# Authority

**This section includes:**

- How Mark's Gospel came to be written
- What does Mark's Gospel mean to Christians?
- The Jews and the Romans
- Religious groups at the time of Jesus

This section deals with background material. The first two units are about the Gospel itself. The writing of books was a rare thing 2000 years ago, since few could read, even fewer could write and every copy of every book had to be written by hand. Yet Mark wrote his Gospel and many copies were made of it. Mark had a clear purpose in writing the Gospel, and Mark's Gospel has been treasured by Christians ever since. What was, and is, so special about this book?

*These units about Mark's Gospel itself cover an important part of the syllabus on which you may well get some questions in your exam.*

The next two units are about the political situation in Palestine at the time of Jesus and about the different aspects of the religious life of the Jewish nation. This is important background material. You will not get questions directly about this part of the syllabus but it is still important that you understand these units, since they will help you understand other subjects later on.

## Key terms

**Christ** The Greek name for the promised leader sent by God (means the same as **Messiah**).

**Gospel** Gospel means 'good news'. The four books in the Bible which are about the life of Jesus are called the four Gospels. When the word is used to mean 'a life of Jesus' or 'the good news about Jesus' it is written 'gospel' with a lower case 'g'. When it is the title of a book it is written 'Gospel' with an upper case 'G'.

## What is a Gospel?

Mark's **Gospel** is one of four books in the Bible about the life of Jesus **Christ**. The four Gospels are very important to Christians because they contain almost everything that is known about Jesus' life and teaching.

The word gospel means good news. Mark did not write what we would call a biography of Jesus. He had a definite, very important aim. He wrote his Gospel to spread the good news about Jesus. He didn't want his readers just to be interested in Jesus. He wanted them to realize that what Jesus said and did affected them.

'The beginning of the Gospel about Jesus Christ, the Son of God.'

This is the opening of Mark's Gospel. These words state that:

- Mark is writing good news
- the good news is about Jesus
- Jesus is the Christ, the promised Messiah
- Jesus is the Son of God.

Jesus said and did many more things than are written in Mark's Gospel. Mark had to choose what to put in and what to leave out.

Mark does not tell us much about other people in the Gospel. He is writing so that his readers will know:

- what Jesus did
- what Jesus said
- who Jesus was/is
- the impact Jesus made on people.

The following passage is a good example of the way in which Mark presents his message.

> When evening came, the boat was in the middle of the lake, and he [Jesus] was alone on land. He saw the disciples straining at the oars, because the wind was against them. About the fourth watch of the night he went out to them, walking on the lake. He was about to pass by them, but when they saw him walking on the lake, they thought he was a ghost. They cried out, because they all saw him and were terrified.
>
> Immediately he spoke to them and said, 'Take courage! It is I. Don't be afraid.' Then he climbed into the boat with them, and the wind died down. They were completely amazed. (6: 47-51)

In this passage:

- Jesus walked on water. Also, the sudden end of the storm was obviously linked in the disciples' minds with Jesus' arrival.
- Jesus said to the disciples 'Take courage! It is I. Don't be afraid.'
- Jesus had the power to walk on water and, apparently, to end the storm as well. He expected his disciples to feel no fear when they were with him, even when the storm seemed dangerous.
- The disciples saw what he had done and were amazed. Events like that made them think 'Who is he? Where does his power come from?'

Mark's Gospel includes many short accounts of events in Jesus' life. The longest section is the description of the events of the twenty-four hours starting with the Last Supper and leading up to the crucifixion. From the start Christians believed that the most important part of Jesus' life was his crucifixion and resurrection.

*The central teaching of Mark's Gospel is that Jesus, the Son of God, died and rose again.*

## Why was it written?

Thousands of people saw what Jesus did and heard what he said. They would have talked about him, and other people would also remember his words and actions. All these people would have been a check on each other's stories. Jesus would have been fresh in all their memories.

At first, as far as we know, nothing was written down. The first Christians believed that Jesus would return and set up the kingdom of God very soon, in their own lifetimes. As time went on, people realized that there was a need for a written account of the life of Jesus because:

- People who had never met Jesus were becoming Christians. Some lived in other countries. They needed to know more about Jesus.
- Jesus' original followers were dying out. They needed to record what Jesus said and did while there were still people who remembered him.

## Who was Mark?

We cannot be absolutely certain who Mark was. Marcus was a common name at the time.

- He could have been the Mark who was a companion of Paul. Paul was an apostle and missionary who carried the gospel to many places where it had never been preached before.
- The Mark who wrote the Gospel could well have been the Mark whom Peter mentions in his first letter (1 Peter 5: 13). Peter was the leader of the disciples. (See page 78)
- We do know that when he wrote his Gospel, Mark got some of his information from Peter. Peter was with Jesus throughout his ministry, so he saw and heard what Jesus did and said.

Papias, who was born about AD 70 and knew the Apostle John, wrote this:

> Mark having become the interpreter of Peter, wrote down accurately whatsoever he remembered. For he neither heard the Lord nor accompanied Him. But afterwards, as I said, he accompanied Peter. Wherefore Mark made no mistake in thus writing some things as he remembered them. For of one thing he took especial care, not to omit anything he had heard, and not to put anything fictitious into the statements.

## *Aramaic words in Mark's Gospel*

Mark wrote his gospel in Greek. Here and there he quotes **Aramaic** words spoken by Jesus. (Aramaic is a language very similar to Hebrew; it was the language spoken by Jesus.) When Jesus raised Jairus' daughter from the dead he said *'Talitha koum'* ('Little girl, I say to you, get up'). On the cross he said *'Eloi, Eloi, lama sabachthani?'* ('My God, my God, why have you forsaken me?') These few Aramaic words, actually spoken by Jesus, indicate that Mark got his information from an eye witness, someone who remembered clearly what Jesus said and did.

### Activities

1. Choose a newspaper article. What does it tell you about the person who wrote it? Give reasons. **PS 2.2, 2.3**

2. Hot seat. The teacher takes the role of Mark. Students ask questions about how and why he wrote his Gospel. **C 1.2a, WO 2.2**

### Key points

- 'Gospel' means 'good news'.
- Mark wrote his Gospel so that people would know who Jesus was and what he did.
- When Mark wrote his Gospel, some eyewitnesses of Jesus were still alive.

# What does Mark's Gospel mean to Christians?

## Christian beliefs about Jesus

Christianity is belief in Jesus Christ. Christians believe Jesus is God the Son. He has always existed. Like God the Father and God the Holy Spirit, Jesus is eternal, without beginning and without end.

Jesus took on human nature, even though he had always existed, he was born as a human being with the same experiences and emotions as other human beings. He lived on earth. He taught about the kingdom of God. He healed people and did many remarkable things. Above all, he died and rose again.

*Everybody stands for the Gospel reading at Mass, a sign of the fact that the life and teaching of Jesus is of supreme importance to Christians.*

Christians believe that their faith is based on events which actually happened. It is important to Christians to know what Jesus said and did. It is important to have accurate, reliable information.

In the Apostles' Creed, Christians say that Jesus suffered under the reign of Pontius Pilate. Pontius Pilate was the Roman governor. A Roman historian called Tacitus wrote about the Christians. He wrote 'Christ, from whom the name was given, had been put to death in the reign of Tiberius by the procurator Pontius Pilate.' Pontius Pilate is named in the Creed to stress that the crucifixion was a historical event – it really happened. The Christian faith depends on the fact that it really happened.

I believe in Jesus Christ, his only Son, our Lord.
He was conceived by the power of the Holy Spirit
and born of the Virgin Mary.
He suffered under Pontius Pilate,
was crucified, died, and was buried.
He descended to the dead.
On the third day he rose again.
He ascended into heaven,
and is seated at the right hand of the Father.
He will come again
to judge the living and the dead.
(The Apostles' Creed)

## Information about Jesus

Christians depend on the four Gospels for information about Jesus. The other books in the New Testament tell us a great deal about why Jesus was so important to his followers. The only accounts of what he actually said and did are the Gospels of Matthew, Mark, Luke and John. These four books have a special significance for Christians. Mark's Gospel is important to Christians because it is one of the four sources of information about the life and teaching of Jesus.

Mark's Gospel is not a biography, a simple account of the life of a man who lived long ago. Mark proclaims that Jesus is Son of God, Messiah, Son of Man, Saviour. That is a dimension to the Gospel which is not part of an ordinary life story.

Mark intended that the Gospel should be read by believers – or people who would become believers.

- A person who believed that Jesus was the Son of God would get the message of the Gospel; a person who did not believe would not see the real point of the book.
- A person with faith would read about the miracles of Jesus and think of them as showing the power of God. A person without faith would think they were rather strange and probably made up.
- A person with faith would understand the parables' teaching about the kingdom of God. A person without faith might not have a clue what the parables meant.

## Is Mark's gospel true?

To Christians, it is vital to know what Jesus did and said. It is important that the Gospels are true. What sort of truth are Christians looking for? Different Christians would answer that question in different ways.

**Fundamentalists** believe that the Bible is completely inspired by God, and cannot contain errors. Where there are apparent contradictions, people do not yet have enough understanding – either of the text or of truth. Fundamentalists accept the miracles just as they are described in the Bible.

**Literalists** are fundamentalists who believe in the exact literal interpretation of scripture. For instance, there are literalists who take 16: 18 literally: 'They will pick up snakes with their hands; and when they drink any deadly poison, it will not hurt them at all.'

**Conservatives** believe that the Bible was inspired by God and the writers wrote what God wanted – they are writing 'the truth' from God for people to understand. The Bible is not a scientific text, and occasionally there may be difficulties with a text where understanding is not clear. They might say that the account of the healing of Legion was basically correct but look for an explanation of what happened to the pigs and why (5: 1-20).

**Liberals** believe that the writers of the Bible were guided by God but because they were human they could make mistakes. Much of the Bible is not intended to be taken literally, but to present spiritual truth using parables, imaginative stories and poetic writing. Liberals might not take the idea of the resurrection of Jesus to mean that the body of Jesus literally was restored to life. To them the presence of Jesus with his followers now is the truth that matters (see page 44).

To fundamentalists it is important that Mark's gospel is true in every way as ordinary fact. To liberals that sort of truth does not matter very much. They are looking for a deeper spiritual truth.

## The Bible – the Word of God

Whether they are literalists, fundamentalists, conservatives, liberals or simply people trying to learn about their faith, Christians believe that the Bible is the Word of God. They believe that there is a message and meaning in the Bible which is as relevant in the twenty-first century as at any other time in history.

Sometimes they find a message for the modern world, God's Word for the whole of society. Sometimes they find a simple message of guidance and comfort for themselves, a Word from God personally for them.

### Activities

1  Imagine an ordinary Christian reading 9: 33-7. What meaning for the present day might that person find in those verses? **PS 2.1, 2.3**

2  Read about the Raising of Jairus' daughter (5: 21-4, 35-43). How might different Christians explain what happened? **PS 2.1, 2.3**

### Key points

- A gospel is not an ordinary life story. It proclaims that Jesus is the Son of God.
- The gospels are very precious to Christians.
- Different Christians understand the Bible in different ways.
- Christians believe that the Bible is as relevant today as it ever was.

# The Jews and the Romans

In order to study Mark's Gospel it is important to know something about events in Palestine at the time.

## The Promised Land

For the Jewish people, Palestine has always been the 'Promised Land'. The Old Testament teaches that the land of Canaan, later known as Palestine, was promised to Abraham by God. It was to be a land in which his descendants would multiply, a witness to other nations of the power and love of God. The Israelites, an early name for the Jews, were God's chosen people, and Palestine was their God-given land.

In the early days of Judaism, the religion was unique among the other religions of the world.

- The Jews believed in the existence of one God, who would stand no rivals, and worshipped him alone.
- The Jews believed that, as descendants of Abraham, they had been chosen by God from all the peoples of the world.

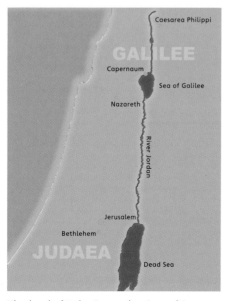

*The land of Palestine at the time of Jesus.*

- They had a unique relationship with God, a **covenant** relationship. God promised to guide and protect the Jews. In return, the Jews were to honour God alone and obey his commands.

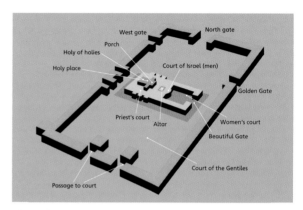

*This is the temple that Jesus would have known. It was the centre of Jewish worship for Jews throughout the world.*

## The temple

At the centre of the worshipping life of the Jews was the temple in Jerusalem. This was the house of God, the visible sign of the presence of God among his people. King Solomon, a great king who lived around 970 BCE, built the first temple, a magnificent building representing the glory and power of God. This temple was destroyed by the Babylonians in 586 BCE. Later a second, less grand, temple was built. Herod the Great began a third temple in 20 BCE. This was a magnificent and huge building, and was the temple of Jesus' day. It was not completed until AD 64, and was destroyed by the Romans in AD 70. There has not been a temple in Jerusalem since that time.

The temple of Jesus' day was the centre of worship for Jews all over the world.

- It was the 'house' of the Lord God.
- The Holy of Holies at the heart of the temple was the place where God was thought to be uniquely present.
- At the entrance to the Holy of Holies was the veil of the temple. Only the high priest could go beyond that point.
- It was the only place where sacrifices of lambs or birds could be offered to God.

It was the place to which all Jewish people, wherever they lived, tried to go at least once a year. Attendance at the temple was particularly important during the Jewish festival of Pesach, or **Passover**. This is the time when Jews remember the Exodus, and give thanks for God's protection and guidance during the 40 years of wilderness wanderings.

Visitors to Jerusalem today can still see the Western Wall, which is all that remains of the Temple that Jesus would have known. It is often called 'The Wailing Wall', as Jewish pilgrims to Jerusalem mourn the loss of the Temple in their prayers at the wall. Jewish sacrificial worship ended with the destruction of Herod's Temple.

## The synagogue

The **synagogue** became the main place of worship after the destruction of the temple. The word 'synagogue' means 'meeting' or 'assembly', and there was a synagogue in every Jewish village or town.

The synagogue continues to be important in the worshipping life of Jews to the present day.

## Roman occupation

Roman armies entered Palestine around 63 BCE. The land was conquered and it became part of the Roman Empire. Palestine, along with most of the known world at the time, was now ruled by the Roman Emperor. This was a tremendous blow to the Jews. Their God-given land had been taken over by a people who did not believe in God. It was an invasion which threatened their whole way of life. The fate of God's chosen people was in the hands of foreigners.

Once the land of Palestine was safely in Roman hands Herod the Great, whose ancestry was partly Jewish, was allowed to reign as a 'puppet king'. Although he was given the title King, real power lay with the Roman Emperor. Herod was very unpopular among the Jews because he was not against the Roman occupation, and was prepared to carry out the Emperor's plans for Palestine. He was on the throne of Palestine when Jesus was born.

When Herod died, the Romans divided Palestine amongst his three sons – Antipas, Archelaus and Philip.

Archelaus' cruelty led to him being replaced by a series of Roman governors, or procurators. Pontius Pilate was appointed to this position in AD 26.

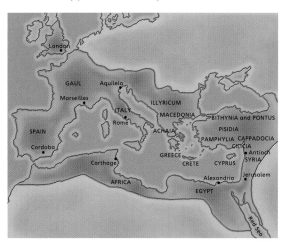

*At the time of Jesus, a significant amount of the world was ruled by the Roman Emperor.*

### Activities

1 Read Psalm 137. Written to recall the time when the Jews were living in exile in Babylon, what does it say about the effect the destruction of Jerusalem and the temple had on the exiled Jews? **PS 2.1**

2 Visit the websites www.templemount.org and www.aish.com/wallcam/ to see what you can discover about the temple at Jerusalem. **IT 2.1, 2.2**

### Key points

- The Jews believe that their God is the one true God.
- God made a covenant with the Jews.
- The land of Palestine is their God-given land.
- The temple was the place where God, uniquely, was to be found. It was at the worshipping heart of the Jews.
- The synagogue became the main place of worship after the destruction of the Temple.
- It greatly offended the Jews that their God-given land was ruled by the Romans, foreigners who did not believe in God.

During his ministry, Jesus came into contact with a number of leading Jewish groups. Most of them looked upon Jesus as a threat to their religion and their way of life. Mark describes a number of occasions when they questioned Jesus' authority to say and do the things he did (for example, the healing of the paralyzed man, 2: 1-12). At times they also set out to trick him into saying something that would damage his ministry or get him into serious trouble with the authorities (for example, asking a question about rising from death, 12: 18-27).

## The Sadducees

The Sadducees were a party of priests. Apart from being very wealthy and having a high position in Jewish society, the Sadducees controlled:

- worship in the temple
- all sacrificial offerings to God
- all temple finances.

The Sadducees were the only religious party who were content to work in partnership with the Romans. They had been given a great deal of freedom to govern the religious lives of the Jews, and they wanted this to continue.

This religious group believed that the **Torah** (the Jewish Law) contained all God's teachings on how to live a proper religious and moral life. They did not believe in a life after death. Nor did they believe that God would send a Messiah.

### Why did they see Jesus as a threat?

Many Jews at the time of Jesus were waiting for a Messiah who would free them from the Romans. On the other hand, the Sadducees enjoyed a comfortable way of life which depended on them keeping religious peace among the Jews. They saw Jesus as a threat because some of his supporters claimed he was the Messiah. They feared he might lead the people to revolt against the Romans. This would endanger the Sadducees' position of power and had to be avoided.

Also, Jesus questioned their authority over temple worship (11: 15-18), and dared to add extra teachings to the Law of Moses. He was therefore a threat to their security and a blasphemer.

## The Pharisees

Most Jews worshipped, not at the temple in Jerusalem but in the local synagogue. The religious group with the greatest influence in the synagogues was the Pharisees. The Pharisees were devoted to keeping the Law of Moses, and they felt that it was their responsibility to help the Jewish people to keep the Law. So they created many interpretations of each of the Commandments God had given to Moses. This was particularly true when it came to the laws surrounding washing, eating, festivals and the Sabbath. The Jewish people were expected to carry out these interpretations in their daily lives. In this way the Pharisees had a great influence on the daily lives of the Jewish people.

The word 'Pharisee' means 'separated one'. Pharisees felt that it was important to separate themselves from foreigners and the outcasts of Jewish society. In doing this, they believed that they could concentrate on obeying the laws of God and remain clean and pure in the eyes of God. The Pharisees believed that God would send a Messiah to guide the Jewish nation back to the ways of God. They also believed in life after death.

*The synagogue is at the centre of every Jewish community.*

## The Scribes

The first scribes were men whose task was to make copies of the Scriptures, written clearly and without error. As the centuries passed, they became experts on Jewish Law and would produce their own interpretations of the Scriptures.

## Why did the Pharisees and Scribes see Jesus as a threat?

The Pharisees and Scribes believed that Jesus was undermining their work. He seemed to ignore many of their interpretations. For example:

- in their view, Jesus and his disciples did not keep the Sabbath (2: 23-8, 3: 1-6), see pages 90–1
- his disciples ate without first washing their hands according to the Pharisees' traditions (7: 1-5)
- his teachings suggested that Jews should concentrate on loving God and their neighbours, rather than on the laws they had created.

Jesus was concerned that the Pharisees had created so many interpretations surrounding the Commandments of God that following them had become a burden to the Jewish people. The Pharisees were in a position to care for the religious needs of the Jews but Jesus felt they had abused their position.

Mark suggests that the Pharisees began looking into Jesus' background and authority almost as soon as he began his ministry. They soon came to the conclusion that he was a dangerous threat and made plans to have him executed (3: 1-6).

## The Sanhedrin

The Sanhedrin was the supreme court of Jewish Law in Israel. The term 'Sanhedrin' means 'council', and it had the power to:

- pass religious laws
- judge and punish those who broke the Law of Moses
- assist the Romans in maintaining law and order among the people.

The Sanhedrin was made up of 70 leading men from Jewish society, under the chairmanship of the High Priest. The members of the Council included chief priests (mostly Sadducees), Pharisees, scribes and Elders (leading Jewish citizens).

When the Romans conquered Palestine, the Sanhedrin was allowed to keep most of its power and authority. However, the right to execute someone who had seriously broken the Law of Moses was taken away. If the Sanhedrin judged that an individual's crime deserved the death penalty, the case had to be taken to the Roman Procurator. He alone could authorize the execution. This is the reason why Jesus was taken to Pontius Pilate early in the morning on the day of his crucifixion (see page 30–1).

The Sanhedrin was disbanded in AD 70 after the destruction of Jerusalem.

### Activities

1 Imagine you are a Sadducee or a Pharisee. Working with a partner, write about 150 words explaining why Jesus' teaching and actions upset you so much. **WO 2.1, 2.2**

2 Hot Seat. A student chooses one of the Ten Commandments and, Pharisee-style, explains it, e.g. the commandment 'Honour your father and your mother'. The rest ask for definitions and rulings. Others ask questions such as 'What if your parents regularly come home drunk? What if they tell you to be home by 8.30 p.m. every night?' **C 2.1a, 2.1b**

### Key points

- The Sadducees were a party of priests at the temple in Jerusalem. They were content to co-operate with the Romans.
- The Pharisees believed in the Law of Moses and interpreted it to show the way it should be followed in everyday life.
- The Sanhedrin, the religious council of the Jews, was the highest authority for the administration of the Jewish Law.

# Exam questions to practise

Below are some sample exam questions on Mark's Gospel. The first three have examiner's tips to give you some hints on how to score full marks. The others are for you to try on your own. A good idea is to work out your own hints on how to score full marks before answering them.

**1** Different Christians mean different things when they say that the Bible is the Word of God.
   **a)** What do fundamentalist Christians mean when they say the Bible is the Word of God? (4)
   **b)** What do Liberal Christians mean when they say the Bible is the Word of God? (4)

**2** Read Mark 6: 30-44 (the Feeding of the 5000, pages 18–19) and answer the questions which follow.

How might this passage be understood by
   **a)** fundamentalist Christians? (3)
   **b)** liberal Christians? (3)

**3** 'Without the Gospels there could be no Christian faith.' Do you agree? Give reasons for your answer, showing that you have thought of more than one point of view. (5)

Now try these questions with no hints. Before you write an answer try to write down your own hints on how to score full marks.

**4** Why did Mark write his Gospel? (4)

**5** 'The Bible is a source of comfort and encouragement to Christians.'
Do you agree? Give reasons for your answer showing that you have thought of more than one point of view. (5)

## How to score full marks

The examiner will be marking on the basis of levels of response (see page vi), so make sure your responses are full and accurate.

**1** This is a question to test what you know. Make sure you describe clearly what each group believes. If you are not sure of the answer pages 4 and 5 should help you.

**2** This is a question to test that you understand the difference between the fundamentalist Christians and liberal Christians. To answer this you need to apply each set of beliefs to the verses you have been given.

**3** This is an evaluation question to make you think and to test how well you can assess a problem or situation. Look for arguments **for and against** the statement you have to discuss. No more than three marks would be given to a response which only looked at one side of the question.

Note that in an examination you might simply be asked to give one or two examples of different ways in which Christians interpret the Bible. If you do, give clear examples by naming the examples you have chosen (e.g. fundamentalists and liberals) and describing each one clearly.

# The person of Jesus

**This section includes**

- Who was Jesus?
- Son of God
- Son of Man
- Jesus, Saviour
- Christ, Messiah, Son of David
- The relevance of Jesus for Christians today

In this section you will learn about what Mark's Gospel says about why Jesus was and is important to Christians. From the very start, people who met Jesus found themselves asking 'Who is he?' Through his teaching and his actions Jesus aimed to show them who he was.

People turned to the scriptures and found there some titles of leaders who, they believed, would one day come from God. Jesus based much of his teaching on the scriptures. What people expected and what Jesus wanted them to see in him were different things.

## Key terms

**Son of David** A title for the Messiah, who would be descended from King David and would, like him, be a great leader.

**Son of God** A title given to Jesus emphasizing that he always existed, in the presence of the Father, before his birth at Bethlehem.

**Son of Man** A heavenly being with special authority from God.

People saw and heard Jesus and asked…

> 'What is this? A new teaching – and with authority! (1: 27)
> 'Who is this? Even the wind and the waves obey him!' (4: 41)
> 'Are you the Christ, the Son of the Blessed One?' (14: 61)

'Who is he?' 'Who are you?' Everyone who met Jesus, anyone who heard of what he said and did, was faced with that question.

The Jews were expecting God to send someone to them. As they thought about Jesus, they found themselves asking 'Is this the person we have been waiting for?'

## What did the Jews expect?

A number of ideas were floating around at the time of Jesus. Some of those ideas were rather vague – it is difficult to understand exactly what they mean. Probably different people thought of them in different ways. In one way or another those ideas show the hopes people had for the future.

### Messiah

People were expecting a Messiah, a leader sent from God. The words Messiah and Christ mean 'anointed one'. In the Old Testament times, kings and high priests were anointed as a sign that they were chosen and set aside by God. As time went on, the idea spread that one day an Anointed One would appear as a leader. Just what exactly people were expecting is hard to know.

- The Messiah would be a **Son of David**. David lived a thousand years before the birth of Jesus. He was the greatest of the kings of Israel. People looked back to his reign as a golden age. The Messiah would be a Son of David in two ways:
  – a descendant of David
  – a great king as David had been.

- The **Zealots** were Jewish freedom fighters. They were looking for a political leader. They hated being ruled by the Romans. They wanted a leader who would restore Israel as a free, independent state. They wanted a warrior.

- Others expected a spiritual leader who would bring in a time of peace. They found support for their hopes in the words of ancient prophets, such as Isaiah.

The Messiah would, of course, be human. The idea that he would be God in human form was totally against what Jews believed – there was only one God. Anyone who claimed to be God was guilty of blasphemy. Blasphemy is speaking insultingly about God or taking God's name in vain.

## Son of Man

The expression **'Son of Man'** is found in the book of Daniel.

> There before me was one like a son of man, coming with the clouds of heaven. He approached the Ancient of Days and was led into his presence.
> He was given authority, glory and sovereign power; all peoples, nations and men of every language worshipped him.
> (Daniel 7: 13-14)

*The Ancient of Days as pictured by William Blake.*

Other Jewish writers used this same idea of the Son of Man with a special authority from God.

# How did Jesus see his mission?

Jesus used ideas about the leader who would come from God. He did not always use them in the way in which they were generally understood.

## Messiah

Jesus did not use the title Messiah himself, though he did accept it when others used it.

When Jesus spoke about kingship, he did not speak of himself as king. Instead, he spoke about the kingdom of God. That kingdom was present on earth in a special way because he himself had come. The first words of Jesus in Mark's Gospel are:

> 'The time has come. The kingdom of God is near. Repent and believe the good news!'
> (1: 15)

In Luke's Gospel (4: 16-21) there is a description of a time when Jesus visited Nazareth. He went to the synagogue and was invited to read from the book of Isaiah.

> 'The Spirit of the Lord is on me, because he has anointed me to preach good news to the poor. He has sent me to proclaim freedom for the prisoners and recovery of sight for the blind, to release the oppressed, to proclaim the year of the Lord's favour.'

When he had finished the reading he said to the congregation, 'Today this scripture is fulfilled in your hearing.' He was stating that he was the Messiah – and showing what he wanted them to understand about the Messiah.

## Son of God

Jesus made quite clear that he was the **Son of God**. He knew that this would offend against the fundamental Jewish belief that there is only one God.

- Mark's Gospel records events which, for Christians, show Jesus being recognized by God the Father as his Son.

- Son of God was not a title Jesus encouraged people to use. 'Whenever the evil spirits saw him, they fell down before him and cried out, "You are the Son of God." But he gave them strict orders not to tell who he was.' (3: 11-12)

- When he was directly challenged by the High Priest to say if he was the Son of God Jesus replied firmly 'I am'. He did so even though he knew that he would be open to a charge of blasphemy.

- When Jesus said he was the Son of God, he added immediately that he was the Son of Man.

## Son of Man

Jesus did speak of himself as Son of Man. He took the idea found in Daniel of a human being with a special authority from God. He said the Son of Man had authority to forgive sins (2: 10f). He said that the Son of Man was Lord of the Sabbath – God's holy day. He added the idea that the Son of Man would suffer, die and rise again.

### Activities

1. Read Isaiah 11: 1-9 and Isaiah 32: 1-8. What sort of Messiah is described in these passages? **PS 2.1, 2.3**

2. Read the verses from Daniel printed above. What picture of the Son of Man is given in this passage? **PS 2.1, 2.3**

### Key points

- At the time of Jesus, Jews were expecting the Messiah, a leader sent from God.

- The Book of Daniel in the Old Testament, and some later writings as well, mention a being called Son of Man.

- Jesus used these ideas in talking about who he was.

- Jesus made clear he was the Son of God – which to many people meant he was guilty of blasphemy.

# Son of God

## Key terms

**Baptism** To dip in or pour water on as a sign of admission into the Christian community.

**Glory** The quality which humans can sense that sets God apart from and above them.

**Holy Spirit** The third person of the Trinity. Christians believe the Holy Spirit is always with them, giving them strength and support.

**Transfiguration** The occasion when Jesus was seen in glory with Moses and Elijah.

**Trinity** Christians think of God as being three Persons but only one God. The three Persons are the Father, the Son and the Holy Spirit.

## Three persons, one God

- The opening words of Mark's Gospel are 'The beginning of the gospel about Jesus Christ, the Son of God.' Mark makes clear from the very start that belief in Jesus as the Son of God is at the heart of the Gospel.

- Christians believe there is only one God. There are three persons, Father, Son and Holy Spirit, but they are not divided; there is only one God.

- Jews believe there is only one God. To the Jews who lived at the time of Jesus, any suggestion that Jesus was the Son of God was blasphemy.

Two of the passages in this unit describe occasions when people heard the voice of God the Father from heaven declaring Jesus to be his Son.

## The baptism

At that time Jesus came from Nazareth in Galilee and was **baptized** by John in the Jordan. As Jesus was coming up out of the water, he saw heaven being torn open and the Spirit descending on him like a dove. And a voice came from heaven: 'You are my Son, whom I love; with you I am well pleased.' (1: 9-11)

- Note that this is the first occasion on which Jesus appears in Mark's Gospel. Mark simply mentions that Jesus was baptized, with no comment on the meaning of his baptism. The point of the event for Mark is the endorsement of Jesus by the Father.

- All three persons of the **Trinity** are present here. The Father speaks, the Son comes from the Jordan, the **Holy Spirit** is seen descending in the form of a dove. The presence of the Father and Spirit endorse Jesus as the Son of God.

See page 106 on baptism for further comment on this passage.

*Christians use many symbols to represent the Trinity.*

*St Patrick used the shamrock as a symbol of the Trinity – Three Persons, One God.*

*Three yet one, inseparable.*

## The Transfiguration

The **Transfiguration** occurred just six days after Jesus was recognized as Messiah by Peter. On that occasion Jesus told the disciples not to tell others that he was the Messiah (see 8: 27-33). The question still had to be answered, 'Who is Jesus?'

Jesus took Peter, James and John with him and led them up a high mountain, where they were all alone. There he was transfigured before them. His clothes became dazzling white, whiter than anyone in the world could bleach them. And there appeared before them Elijah and Moses, who were talking with Jesus. Peter said to Jesus, 'Rabbi, it is good for us to be here. Let us put up three shelters – one for you, one for Moses and one for Elijah.' (He did not know what to say, they were so frightened.) Then a cloud appeared and enveloped them, and a voice came from the cloud: 'This is my Son, whom I love. Listen to him!' Suddenly, when they looked round, they no longer saw anyone with them except Jesus. (9: 2-8)

- Jesus was transfigured. Mark says he was seen in **glory**. He appeared in a way which the disciples had never seen before. It was not just that his clothes were shining white. There was something about his presence that seemed wonderful in a way that they could not understand. The disciples were convinced he had an authority that was more than human. They were filled with awe. Mark clearly believed they had experienced the glory of God.

- Jesus appeared with Moses and Elijah. These two men represented the Jewish religion, based on the Law and the Prophets. Both had been dead for hundreds of years, yet here they were speaking with Jesus. Moses was the great law-giver; he himself had received the Ten Commandments from God on Mount Sinai. Elijah was the greatest of the prophets. Indeed, Malachi had apparently foretold that Elijah would appear before the coming of the Messiah, to prepare the way for him. Jesus could have no greater supporters of his divine authority than these two men.

- The disciples were overawed by their experience. Peter asked if they should put up shelters for Jesus, Moses and Elijah – a suggestion which sounds like the words of someone who does not really know what is happening or what he should say.

- A voice from heaven was heard: 'This is my Son, whom I love. Listen to him!' Peter, James and John were convinced that the voice could only be that of God the Father.

## Jesus' trial

After the Last Supper Jesus and the eleven disciples went to the Garden of Gethsemane, where Jesus was arrested. He was taken to the high priest and put on trial. The trial is described in 14: 53-65, see page 28.

The critical point in the trial came when the high priest asked Jesus, 'Are you the Christ, the Son of the Blessed One?' Jesus answered, 'I am, and you will see the Son of Man sitting at the right hand of the Mighty One and coming on the clouds of heaven.'

Jesus had said he was the Son of God. For saying that, he was condemned as guilty of blasphemy. The verdict was that he was guilty and deserved to die.

### Activities

1 Read again the account of Jesus' baptism. What thoughts might have been going through Jesus' mind as he stepped out of the water? PS 2.1

2 Thought-tracking: Peter, James and John are looking at Jesus and his companions on the mountain of Transfiguration. What are Peter, James and John saying and thinking? PS 2.1, 2.2, C 2.1a, 2.1b

### Key points

- From his first verse Mark states that Jesus is the Son of God.
- At Jesus' baptism and Transfiguration a voice from heaven announced that he was the Son of God.
- At his trial in front of the high priest Jesus said plainly that he was the Son of God.

# Son of Man

**Faith** Belief and trust which is so complete that it involves following the person in whom you place your trust.

## A heavenly being

Jesus often used the term Son of Man when speaking of himself. He and his followers would think of the Son of Man as the being with heavenly authority described in the Book of Daniel. This unit looks at some of the occasions when Jesus called himself the Son of Man and thinks about what he meant.

### The paralyzed man

A few days later, when Jesus again entered Capernaum, the people heard that he had come home. So many gathered that there was no room left, not even outside the door, and he preached the word to them. Some men came, bringing to him a paralytic, carried by four of them. Since they could not get him to Jesus because of the crowd, they made an opening in the roof above Jesus and, after digging through it, lowered the mat the paralyzed man was lying on. When Jesus saw their faith, he said to the paralytic, 'Son, your sins are forgiven.'

Now some teachers of the law were sitting there, thinking to themselves, 'Why does this fellow talk like that? He's blaspheming! Who can forgive sins but God alone?'

Immediately Jesus knew in his spirit that this was what they were thinking in their hearts, and he said to them, 'Why are you thinking these things? Which is easier: to say to the paralytic, "Your sins are forgiven," or to say, "Get up, take your mat and walk"? But that you may know that the Son of Man has authority on earth to forgive sins...' He said to the paralytic, 'I tell you, get up, take your mat and go home.' He got up, took his mat and walked out in full view of them all. This amazed everyone and they praised God, saying, 'We have never seen anything like this!' (2: 1-12)

- The four friends had tremendous faith. They were determined to get their paralyzed friend to Jesus. Lowering him through the roof was a drastic way of setting about it! The flat roof was probably made of beams and rafters across which matting, branches and twigs were laid, with dried earth, trodden down hard, on top. Even then, it must be hoped that it could easily be repaired!

- Jesus saw their **faith**. His reaction was to say to the invalid, 'Your sins are forgiven'.

- Jesus' words cause consternation. Blasphemy! Only God can forgive sins. He is claiming to be God.

- No one said anything. Jesus knew what they are thinking. He asked them, 'Which is easier – to say "Your sins are forgiven" or to say "Get up and walk"? It was just as easy to say the one as the other. To do either – that was a different matter. Only God could forgive sins. It would take the power of God to cure a paralyzed man by just saying the word. Either way, it needed the authority and power of God.

- What Jesus said next is the key to the whole passage. 'But that you may know that the Son of Man has authority on earth to forgive sins...' Jesus could both forgive the man's sins and heal him through the power of God.

- Jesus used the title Son of Man. The Son of Man had the power of forgiveness and healing.

*The paralyzed man could have been lowered into a flat-roofed house such as this.*

## The request of James and John

James and John, the sons of Zebedee, came to Jesus. 'Teacher,' they said, 'we want you to do for us whatever we ask.'

'What do you want me to do for you?' he asked.

They replied, 'Let one of us sit at your right and the other at your left in your glory.'

'You don't know what you are asking,' Jesus said. 'Can you drink the cup I drink or be baptized with the baptism I am baptized with?'

'We can,' they answered.

Jesus said to them, 'You will drink the cup I drink and be baptized with the baptism I am baptized with, but to sit at my right or left is not for me to grant. These places belong to those for whom they have been prepared.'

When the ten heard about this, they became indignant with James and John. Jesus called them together and said, 'You know that those who are regarded as rulers of the Gentiles lord it over them, and their high officials exercise authority over them. Not so with you. Instead, whoever wants to become great among you must be your servant, and whoever wants to be first must be slave of all. For even the Son of Man did not come to be served, but to serve, and to give his life as a ransom for many.' (10: 35-45)

- Jesus told the disciples about the importance of serving others.
- Once again, he used the title Son of Man. The life of the Son of Man would be a ransom. In other words, there was a special, unique quality about the Son of Man. The death of Jesus would mean eternal life for many.

## The prediction of the passion

Jesus began to teach his disciples that the Son of Man must suffer many things and be rejected by the elders, chief priests and teachers of the law, and that he must be killed and after three days rise again. He spoke plainly about this, and Peter took him aside and began to rebuke him.

But when Jesus turned and looked at his disciples, he rebuked Peter. 'Get behind me, Satan!' he said. 'You do not have in mind the things of God, but the things of men.' (8: 31-3)

- Immediately before Jesus spoke these words, Peter had said that he believed Jesus was the Messiah (see page 20). Jesus' reaction is not to talk about being the Messiah but about his future suffering. This is the first time, in Mark's Gospel, that the idea that Jesus would suffer is mentioned.

- Jesus did not simply say that the Son of Man *would* suffer. He said that the Son of Man *must* suffer. It was his destiny.

- Jesus also said that he would rise again. In Mark's Gospel, this is the first hint of the resurrection.

- Peter's reaction was natural enough. He took Jesus aside for a quiet word. Jesus rebuked him firmly. He went on to say that anyone who wanted to follow him had to be prepared for suffering. Note verses 34-8 (see pages 74–5 on Discipleship) and the words to James and John above. (8: 31-3)

### Activities

1 Was there anything wrong in what James and John asked? Was there anything wrong in the reaction of the other ten disciples? What is a ransom? What could Jesus have meant by saying his life was a ransom for many? **PS 2.1**

2 Thought-tracking: on the prediction of the passion (8: 31-3); students take the roles of Jesus, Peter and another disciple. **C 2.1a, 2.1b**

### Key points

- 'Son of Man' is the title Jesus used most often when speaking of himself.
- 'Son of Man' refers to a being who is more than human. The Son of Man has power and authority which can only come from God.

# Jesus, Saviour

## The name 'Jesus'

The name 'Jesus' means Saviour. In Matthew's Gospel we read that Joseph was told, 'You are to give him the name Jesus, because he will save his people from their sins.' (Matthew 1: 21) 'Jesus' was quite a common name at the time. In his letter to the Colossians, Paul sends greetings to the Christians in Colossi from 'Jesus who is called Justus'.

The three passages examined in this section emphasise the impact Jesus made on people.

## The calming of the storm

When evening came, Jesus said to his disciples, 'Let us go over to the other side.' Leaving the crowd behind, they took him along, just as he was, in the boat. There were also other boats with him. A furious squall came up, and the waves broke over the boat, so that it was nearly swamped. Jesus was in the stern, sleeping on a cushion. The disciples woke him and said to him, 'Teacher, don't you care if we drown?'

He got up, rebuked the wind and said to the waves, 'Quiet! Be still!' Then the wind died down and it was completely calm.

He said to his disciples, 'Why are you so afraid? Do you still have no faith?'

They were terrified and asked each other, 'Who is this? Even the wind and the waves obey him!' (4: 35-41)

A storm over the Sea of Galilee.

- Why did the disciples wake Jesus? Did they expect him to help cope with the boat? There is no hint that they expected him to save them in the way that he did.

- After Jesus had calmed the storm with a few words, he asked the disciples why they were afraid. He expected them to have faith in him.

- Even when the storm was over, the disciples were terrified. The fear they felt was not a fear of physical harm. What they experienced is awe.

In his description of the calming of the storm Mark showed Jesus' power over nature. The following miracle also shows the power of Jesus over the natural order of things.

## The feeding of the 5000

The apostles gathered around Jesus and reported to him all they had done and taught. Then, because so many people were coming and going that they did not even have a chance to eat, he said to them, 'Come with me by yourselves to a quiet place and get some rest.' So they went away by themselves in a boat to a solitary place. But many who saw them leaving recognised them and ran on foot from all the towns and got there ahead of them. When Jesus landed and saw a large crowd, he had compassion on them, because they were like sheep without a shepherd. So he began teaching them many things. By this time it was late in the day, so his disciples came to him. 'This is a remote place,' they said, 'and it's already very late. Send the people away so they can go to the surrounding countryside and villages and buy themselves something to eat.' But he answered, 'You give them something to eat.'

They said to him, 'That would take eight months of a man's wages! Are we to go and spend that much on bread and give it to them to eat?'

'How many loaves do you have?' he asked. 'Go and see.' When they found out, they said, 'Five – and two fish.'

Then Jesus directed them to have all the people sit down in groups on the green grass. So they sat down in groups of hundreds and fifties. Taking the five loaves and the two fish and looking up to heaven, he gave thanks and broke the loaves. Then he gave them to his disciples to set before the people. He also divided the two fish among them all. They all ate and were satisfied, and the disciples picked up twelve basketfuls of broken pieces of bread and fish. The number of the men who had eaten was five thousand. (6: 30-44)

- The impact Jesus was making on people is very clear here. Crowds were determined to see Jesus and to listen to him.

- Jesus saw the crowds. His reaction to them was compassion. He saw their need. He taught them – and they listened.

- Apparently the disciples did not expect Jesus to do anything but send the people away. They did not expect him to feed them.

- The description of what happened next is very detailed. The account includes:

  1 what the cost of feeding the people would be
  2 the precise amount of food that they had
  3 the way in which the people were told to arrange themselves – even that the grass was green (not always the case in Israel)
  4 Jesus giving thanks before breaking the bread
  5 the number of people who were fed – and the amount of food left over.

The third of the passages which shows the extraordinary power of Jesus concerns a woman who was not a Jew – but who had faith in Jesus.

### The Syro-Phoenician woman's daughter

Jesus went to the vicinity of Tyre. He entered a house and did not want anyone to know it; yet he could not keep his presence secret. In fact, as soon as she heard about him, a woman whose little daughter was possessed by an evil spirit came and fell at his feet. The woman was a Greek, born in Syrian Phoenicia. She begged Jesus to drive the demon out of her daughter.

'First let the children eat all they want,' he told her, 'for it is not right to take the children's bread and toss it to their dogs.'

'Yes, Lord,' she replied, 'but even the dogs under the table eat the children's crumbs.'

Then he told her, 'For such a reply, you may go; the demon has left your daughter.' She went home and found her child lying on the bed, and the demon gone. (7: 24-30)

- Jesus had gone out of Jewish territory into the area round Tyre. The people living here were gentiles (non-Jews), but they had obviously heard of Jesus.

- In replying to the woman, Jesus used 'children' to mean 'Jews' and 'dogs' to mean 'gentiles'. He was telling her that he should use his power first for the Jews, God's chosen people. He was testing her faith – perhaps with a faint smile as he did so.

- The woman was not to be put off. With her faith and her love of her daughter, she replied in the same spirit. Jesus praised her faith.

- Jesus cured her daughter – without seeing her.

### Activities

1 Some people think that the description of the calming of the storm includes one or two details which seem to have come from Peter, the eye-witness who supplied Mark with much of the information in the gospel. Can you find any such details in the passage? **PS 2.1**

2 Forum theatre: Jesus and the Syro-Phoenician woman.
**C 2.1a, PS 2.2, 2.3, WO 2.2, 2.3**

### Key points

- The name Jesus means Saviour.
- Jesus used his power to save people from danger, hunger and illness.
- Above all, Christians believe that Jesus saves them from sin and hell.

## What did Jesus mean by Messiah?

Mark meant his readers to understand that Jesus was the Messiah. But what Jesus meant by Messiah and what the majority of ordinary people meant by Messiah were two different things.

- Jesus wanted people to know he was the Messiah – so long as they had the right idea about Messiahship.

- The problem was that people were looking for a Messiah who would be the ruler of an earthly kingdom. Jesus was not that sort of Messiah.

- Jesus had a mission to draw people into the kingdom of God. People had to see the Messiah as bringing in the kingdom of God.

As you read the three passages which follow, see how the idea of Messiahship appears in each event. Before doing so, read the unit on the idea of Messiah on pages 12 and 13 again. Remember:

- Messiah and Christ mean the same

- the Messiah would be a descendant of David.

### Caesarea Philippi

Jesus and his disciples went on to the villages around Caesarea Philippi. On the way he asked them, 'Who do people say I am?' They replied, 'Some say John the Baptist; others say Elijah; and still others, one of the prophets.' 'But what about you?' he asked. 'Who do you say I am?' Peter answered, 'You are the Christ.' Jesus warned them not to tell anyone about him. (8: 27-30)

- The passage shows that people were saying Jesus was a holy man, a man of God. John the Baptist, Elijah and the prophets were remembered for preaching the word of God, not as miracle workers. People hadn't made the step of saying Jesus was the Messiah.

- Peter did say, 'You are the Christ'. But, it seems, Peter had not grasped the sort of Messiah Jesus was. After telling them not to tell anyone about him, Jesus told his disciples that the Son of Man must die and rise again (see page 17).

- When Peter said that this should not happen, Jesus turned on him and said 'Get behind me, Satan!' Peter did not see what Jesus meant by Messiah.

- Jesus told them not to tell anyone that he was the Messiah. This is an example of what is called Messianic secrecy. Until his followers did understand, Messiah was not a word Jesus wanted them to use.

### Blind Bartimaeus

Then they came to Jericho. As Jesus and his disciples, together with a large crowd, were leaving the city, a blind man, Bartimaeus (that is, the Son of Timaeus), was sitting by the roadside begging. When he heard that it was Jesus of Nazareth, he began to shout, 'Jesus, Son of David, have mercy on me!' Many rebuked him and told him to be quiet, but he shouted all the more, 'Son of David, have mercy on me!' Jesus stopped and said, 'Call him.' So they called to the blind man, 'Cheer up! On your feet! He's calling you.' Throwing his cloak aside, he jumped to his feet and came to Jesus. 'What do you want me to do for you?' Jesus asked him. The blind man said, 'Rabbi, I want to see.' 'Go,' said Jesus, 'your faith has healed you.' Immediately he received his sight and followed Jesus along the road. (10: 46-52)

- Bartimaeus had heard of Jesus and his miracles. He believed what he had heard. When told Jesus was coming that way that was enough for him! Here at last was a chance to be able to see. No one could shut him up – he was desperate to get Jesus' attention.

- Bartimaeus called Jesus 'Son of David'. To him Jesus was the Messiah.

- Did Jesus have a twinkle in his eye as he asked, 'What do you want me to do for you?' He knew that Bartimaeus wanted to see!

- Your faith has healed you.' Faith was a key factor in the miracles of Jesus (see pages 62–7).

## Entry to Jerusalem

This passage describes how Jesus rode into Jerusalem on a donkey, only five days before he was crucified. This is the event celebrated by Christians on Palm Sunday.

*Palm Sunday procession approaching Jerusalem.*

> As they approached Jerusalem and came to Bethphage and Bethany at the Mount of Olives, Jesus sent two of his disciples, saying to them, 'Go to the village ahead of you, and just as you enter it, you will find a colt tied there, which no-one has ever ridden. Untie it and bring it here. If anyone asks you, "Why are you doing this?" tell him, 'The Lord needs it and will send it back here shortly.''
>
> They went and found a colt outside in the street, tied at a doorway. As they untied it, some people standing there asked, 'What are you doing, untying that colt?'
>
> They answered as Jesus had told them to, and the people let them go. When they brought the colt to Jesus and threw their cloaks over it, he sat on it. Many people spread their cloaks on the road, while others spread branches they had cut in the fields. Those who went ahead and those who followed shouted, 'Hosanna!' 'Blessed is he who comes in the name of the Lord!' 'Blessed is the coming kingdom of our father David!' 'Hosanna in the highest!'
>
> Jesus entered Jerusalem and went to the temple. He looked around at everything, but since it was already late, he went out to Bethany with the Twelve. (11: 1-11)

- Jesus was fulfilling the prophecy of Zechariah. By riding into Jerusalem he was showing that he was the Messiah. He was also showing the sort of Messiah he was – a peaceful Messiah, 'Gentle and riding on a donkey…He will proclaim peace to the nations.'

- 'Blessed is the coming kingdom of our father David!' The people who welcomed Jesus got the message about Jesus being the Messiah. Whether they understood the sort of Messiah he was is a different matter.

- **Hosanna** is a Hebrew word meaning 'Save now'. However, it was often used as a shout of greeting rather than as a cry for help. The words 'Hosanna in the highest' are a shout of greeting and of homage (honour) as well.

The idea that Jesus was the Messiah was seen as a threat by the Jewish religious leaders – who did not understand the sort of Messiah Jesus claimed to be.

### Activities

1. Jesus did not try to stop Bartimaeus calling him Son of David. Why do you think he allowed himself to be recognized as Messiah on this occasion? **PS 2.1**

2. Forum theatre: Jesus riding into Jerusalem accompanied by two or three disciples. Possibilities for intervention from passers-by, Jewish priests, Romans.
   **C 2.1a, PS 2.2, 2.3, WO 2.2, 2.3**

### Key points

- Christians believe Jesus was the Messiah.

- At Caesarea Philippi, Jesus made clear that his followers should not talk of him as Messiah until people understood what sort of Messiah he was.

- Bartimaeus called Jesus 'Son of David' and showed faith in him.

- By his entry into Jerusalem Jesus was showing that he was the Messiah – and the sort of Messiah he was.

## How Christians today think of Jesus

In Mark's Gospel, Jesus spoke of himself in many different ways. Each title had a particular meaning for the people to whom he was speaking. He spoke to them as individuals or as groups, in ways which helped them personally to understand his message.

For centuries Christians have read the Gospels to learn about what Jesus said, taught and did.

The first thing that matters to Christians is that what Jesus said is true. If it is not, then he cannot be relevant to them in the twenty-first century. They accept his words as true. Along with that it is important to them that what was written about him is true. Remember that different Christians (literalists, fundamentalists, conservative and liberal Christians) understand truth in different ways.

The last four sections have been about titles which Mark used when writing about Jesus. Jesus himself either used those titles or showed that he approved of them. All these titles influence the way in which Christians think of Jesus in the twenty-first century.

## Son of God

It is all-important to Christians that Jesus is God the Son. They believe that Jesus has always existed, together with the Father and Holy Spirit.

Jesus was born as a human being to make God known to the human race. At times in his ministry he did things which made people think he must be the Son of God. He said he was the Son of God.

In the first verse of the Gospel, Mark states that Jesus is the Son of God. In the last verse it states that Jesus was with his disciples when they went out to preach after the Ascension. It is important to Christians that Jesus, Son of God, is present with them in their everyday lives.

## Son of Man

Jesus used the title Son of Man more than any other title. He used the title to show that his power and authority came from God. The Son of Man had power to forgive sins (2: 1-12).

The Son of Man was Lord of the Sabbath (2: 23-8). Also, the Son of Man's life was a ransom (10: 45). The Son of Man will be seen on the right hand of God in the clouds of heaven.

Christians do not use the words 'Son of Man' very often when speaking about Jesus. Nonetheless, the ideas behind the phrase are important to them. Christians believe:

- Jesus has God's authority
- Jesus can forgive sins
- Jesus' death means salvation for everyone
- Jesus is with the Father in heaven
- Jesus will come back to earth in glory.

## Saviour

When Christians talk of Jesus as Saviour they mean that:

- human beings sin
- sin deserves punishment
- sin separates people from God
- through Jesus, people are reconciled to God
- Jesus saves people from the consequences of their sins.

It is of great importance to Christians that their sins may be forgiven and that they may be able to be with God when they die. They trust in Jesus as their Saviour, who saves them from sin and offers them forgiveness.

## Messiah, Christ, Son of David

Christians believe that the whole Bible is the word of God. That includes the Old Testament. They look for a link between the Old Testament and the New Testament. Jesus obviously saw himself as being foreshadowed in the Old Testament. Christians believe that Jesus is the Messiah, the Christ, prophesied in the Old Testament. The word 'Christ' is used as a name rather than a title.

In the Old Testament Christians see God making himself known to the human race, preparing them for the time when the Messiah would come. It is central to the New Testament that Jesus is the Messiah.

## Activities

1 In groups of two or three, discuss the illustrations on this page, which show ways in which people of different cultures picture Jesus. In what ways are they alike? In what ways are they different?
**PS2.1, WO2.1, 2.2**

2 Is it easier for Christians to understand the Gospels if they have a mental picture of what Jesus looked like – even if it is the wrong picture? **PS2.1**

## Key points

- It is vital for Christians that they know and understand who Jesus is.
- Modern Christians use the thoughts and ideas used by Jesus and his followers and try to interpret them in a relevant way.
- Sometimes the language used by Jesus is difficult for modern Christians. It is hard to link the words 'Son of Man' with a heavenly being. The things which Jesus taught through the phrase 'Son of Man' are no less important for Christians now.

# Exam questions to practise

Below are some sample exam questions on the person of Jesus. The first two have examiner's tips to give you some hints on how to score full marks. The others are for you to try on your own. A good idea is to work out your own hints on how to score full marks before answering the questions.

1  **(i)** Describe briefly what happened on one occasion when Jesus was called the Son of God. (4)
   **(ii)** Explain why the speaker called Jesus 'Son of God' and why Jesus responded as he did. (4)

2  'I don't know whether Jesus is the Son of God. I don't think it matters. Being a Christian is all about the way you treat other people.'

Do you agree? Give reasons for your answer, showing that you have thought of more than one point of view. (5)

Now try these questions with no hints. Before you write an answer, try to write down your own hints on how to score full marks.

3  **(i)** Describe what happened when Jesus rode into Jerusalem on a donkey. (5)
   **(ii)** Explain why the people who saw Jesus ride into Jerusalem were so excited by what they saw. (3)
   **(iii)** What is the importance of this event to Christians today? (3)

4  Explain the conversation between Jesus and the Syro-Phoenician woman. (6)

## How to score full marks

1  The examiner will be marking on the basis of levels of response in (i), so make sure your responses are full and accurate. It should not make any difference which example you choose. The examiner will give full marks if you give a very full account of a short incident. Full marks will also be given for a less full account of a longer or more difficult incident.

   In (ii) two marks would be given for each part of the response, two marks for a full answer, one for a weaker answer. If you are not sure of how to answer, look back to pages 14–15.

2  This is an evaluation question to make you think and to test how well you can assess a problem or situation. Look for arguments **for and against** the statement you have to discuss. No more than three marks would be given to a response which only looked at one side of the question.

   Note that the question is about how important belief in Jesus is to Christians.

**This section includes:**

- Gethsemane
- The trial before the high priest
- The Roman trial
- The crucifixion
- The death of Jesus
- Why did Jesus die?

In this section you will study the events leading up the crucifixion. The crucifixion and resurrection are central to the Christian faith. Make sure you know what is written in Mark's Gospel about what happened and why it happened.

# Gethsemane

## Key terms

**Crucifixion** Death caused by being fixed to a cross. Christians think above all of the crucifixion of Jesus.

**Resurrection** A restoring of life after death. The word usually refers to Jesus' returning to life after his death on the cross. It is also used to describe Christians coming to life in heaven after they have died.

## The heart of the faith

The death and **resurrection** of Jesus are, for Christians, the most important events that have ever happened. Mark, like the other Gospel writers, describes carefully what happened.

### Jesus prayed

After the Last Supper (see pages 96–7) Jesus took his disciples to a quiet place to pray.

> They went to a place called Gethsemane, and Jesus said to his disciples, 'Sit here while I pray.' He took Peter, James and John along with him, and he began to be deeply distressed and troubled. 'My soul is overwhelmed with sorrow to the point of death,' he said to them. 'Stay here and keep watch.'
>
> Going a little farther, he fell to the ground and prayed that if possible the hour might pass from him. 'Abba, Father,' he said, 'everything is possible for you. Take this cup from me. Yet not what I will, but what you will.'
>
> Then he returned to his disciples and found them sleeping. 'Simon,' he said to Peter, 'are you asleep? Could you not keep watch for one hour? Watch and pray so that you will not fall into temptation. The spirit is willing, but the body is weak.'
>
> Once more he went away and prayed the same thing. When he came back, he again found them sleeping, because their eyes were heavy. They did not know what to say to him.
>
> Returning the third time, he said to them, 'Are you still sleeping and resting? Enough!

> The hour has come. Look, the Son of Man is betrayed into the hands of sinners. Rise! Let us go! Here comes my betrayer!' (14: 32-42)

### Jesus chose to accept crucifixion

- Jesus could have tried to avoid crucifixion. He did not make the attempt. He went consciously and deliberately towards his death, because he believed that he was doing what God wanted.

- Jesus also showed that he had a sense of a special destiny. He referred to himself as the Son of Man, the mysterious being who was described in the Old Testament as being given unique honour and authority. He himself had spoken of the Son of Man as a person who *had* to suffer. It was his destiny.

We can see a conflict in Jesus here:

- Jesus showed that he was aware of a special relationship with God the Father. He addressed God as 'Abba', which is the Aramaic word children would use when talking to their fathers.

- At the same time, he was overwhelmed with fear and grief. He pleaded with the Father that the cup of suffering might leave him – in other words, that he might not have to suffer as he knew he was going to suffer. Perhaps more than anywhere else in the gospel we see Jesus experiencing agony and intense distress like any other human being.

- Jesus wanted to have disciples with him at this tense time of waiting. As on two other important occasions, (see 9: 2–13 and 14: 32–42), he took Peter, James and John aside with him, telling them to watch while he prayed.

- He chose to accept suffering because he was to do what God wanted. In his own words, 'Not what I will, but what you will.'

- In his time of crisis Jesus prayed. When he returned to the disciples and found them asleep he told Peter to pray as well. However, he did not tell Peter to pray for him. Peter was told to pray for himself, that he would not fall into temptation.

## Jesus is arrested

Just as he was speaking, Judas, one of the Twelve, appeared. With him was a crowd armed with swords and clubs, sent from the chief priests, the teachers of the law, and the elders.

Now the betrayer had arranged a signal with them: 'The one I kiss is the man; arrest him and lead him away under guard.' Going at once to Jesus, Judas said, 'Rabbi!' and kissed him. The men seized Jesus and arrested him. Then one of those standing near drew his sword and struck the servant of the high priest, cutting off his ear.

'Am I leading a rebellion,' said Jesus, 'that you have come out with swords and clubs to capture me? Every day I was with you, teaching in the temple courts, and you did not arrest me. But the Scriptures must be fulfilled.' Then everyone deserted him and fled.

A young man, wearing nothing but a linen garment, was following Jesus. When they seized him, he fled naked, leaving his garment behind. (14: 43-52)

- 'A crowd armed with swords and clubs'. Obviously the chief priests expected Jesus and his followers to resist arrest.

- Judas, one of the twelve disciples, was leading the group. He would have known where Jesus would be.

- A kiss was a normal greeting, so, Judas hoped, it would not have been too obvious that he was betraying Jesus.

- 'Am I leading a rebellion?' asked Jesus. The priests were certainly afraid of what might happen if they did not get rid of Jesus. They were also afraid of what might happen if they arrested him when a lot of people were around. See 14: 1-2.

- One of the disciples did try to defend Jesus. When it was obvious that Jesus was not going to resist arrest, they all ran away.

### Activities

1 Look at the picture of Gethsemane. Why did the artist make the setting modern Glasgow rather than Jerusalem? **PS 2.1, 2.3**

2 Visit www.gospelcom.net and look at the sites on the Bible Land Visual Tour which are traditionally linked with the events in Gethsemane and with the trials and crucifixion of Jesus. Do you think it is important to Christians that they can visit places where, it is said, these events in the life of Jesus took place? **IT 2.1, 2.2, PS 2.1**

### Key points

- Jesus knew that he would be arrested but did not try to escape.

- Jesus prayed that, if possible, he might not have to suffer. Yet his prayer ended, 'Not what I will, but what you will.'

- Jesus did not resist arrest.

# The trial before the high priest

## Why was Jesus arrested?

After Jesus had been arrested, he was taken to be tried by the high priest. The priests had taken this drastic action because Jesus seemed to be a real threat to everything they stood for.

- Jesus was a religious threat. The chief priests expected a Messiah to come. They expected a Messiah to approve of them, the religious leaders of the nation, not a Messiah who would challenge and criticize them.

- Jesus was a political danger. He rode into Jerusalem on a donkey – thus claiming to be the Messiah (see page 21). Many people thought of the Messiah as a political leader.

- If Jesus had tried to lead a rebellion, there were plenty of people ready to follow. The chief priests did not want a rebellion. They had learned to live with the Roman rulers.

- The priests were afraid of trouble breaking out among the people if they made a false move when they tried to arrest Jesus.

Now the Passover and the Feast of Unleavened Bread were only two days away, and the chief priests and the teachers of the law were looking for some sly way to arrest Jesus and kill him. 'But not during the Feast,' they said, 'or the people may riot.' (14: 1-2)

They took Jesus to the high priest, and all the chief priests, elders and teachers of the law came together. Peter followed him at a distance, right into the courtyard of the high priest. There he sat with the guards and warmed himself at the fire. The chief priests and the whole Sanhedrin were looking for evidence against Jesus so that they could put him to death, but they did not find any. Many testified falsely against him, but their statements did not agree.

Then some stood up and gave this false testimony against him: 'We heard him say, "I will destroy this man-made temple and in three days will build another, not made by man."' Yet even then their testimony did not agree.

Then the high priest stood up before them and asked Jesus, 'Are you not going to answer? What is this testimony that these men are bringing against you?' But Jesus remained silent and gave no answer. Again the high priest asked him, 'Are you the Christ, the Son of the Blessed One?' 'I am,' said Jesus. 'And you will see the Son of Man sitting at the right hand of the Mighty One and coming on the clouds of heaven.' The high priest tore his clothes. 'Why do we need any more witnesses?' he asked. 'You have heard the blasphemy. What do you think?' They all condemned him as worthy of death. Then some began to spit at him; they blindfolded him, struck him with their fists, and said, 'Prophesy!' And the guards took him and beat him. (14: 53-65)

The trial, as described by Mark, was highly irregular.

- At the start of the trial no formal charge was made for Jesus to answer. Those present were looking for charges to bring against Jesus.

- The person in charge of the trial, along with all the other members of the Sanhedrin, was among those looking for some reason for condemning Jesus. In any trial, the judge and jury should be unbiased.

- The trial was conducted by night, without Jesus having any chance to arrange his defence.

Mark does not draw attention to these points. He is not bothered about the technicalities of the trial. He is only concerned with why Jesus was sentenced.

> **The real issues were:**
> **Who was Jesus?**
> **What right had Jesus to say and do what he did?**
> **What authority did he have?**

Note the following points which Mark does record.

- Some witnesses gave false evidence but they contradicted each other.

- One charge against Jesus was that he had threatened to destroy the temple and build another in three days. Since the temple was the uniquely sacred house of God, the accusation that he had threatened to destroy it was a very serious charge. In John's Gospel it is recorded that Jesus did say 'Destroy the temple and I will raise it again in three days.' John adds, 'But the temple he had spoken of was his body.' In any case, the witnesses did not agree and so the charge could not stand.

- Throughout the accusations Jesus did not defend himself or claim that the charges were false. He did not rise to the bait when the high priest asked him, 'What is this testimony that these men are bringing against you?'

- At last the high priest asked him, 'Are you the Christ, the Son of the Blessed One?' Jesus answered, 'I am.' He went on to say, 'And you will see the Son of Man sitting at the right hand of the Mighty One and coming on the clouds of heaven.'

- Jesus was found guilty of **blasphemy** because he said he was the Son of God.

- Jesus had also said he was the Messiah. That was not in itself an offence, though the high priest would not have believed him.

- The high priest tore his clothes as a sign that Jesus was guilty of blasphemy.

- The Sanhedrin agreed Jesus deserved to be put to death. That was all they could do – they could not order the sentence to be carried out.

- They blindfolded Jesus and struck him, shouting 'Prophesy'. They meant that if Jesus were indeed the Son of God he would know who had hit him because he would know everything.

## Respect for God's name

Here is an extract from an ancient Jewish text describing the way in which a person was put on trial for blasphemy. It shows how reverently the name of God was treated. Only when asked by the judge could a witness use the name. It also shows the way in which the judges would rend (tear) their garments as a sign that the blasphemy had been committed.

> They say to the chief among the witnesses
> 'Say exactly what you heard', and he says it;
> and the judges stand up on their feet and
> rend their garments,
> and they may not mend them again.

## Activities

1  Read again the account of the trial. Look at the way in which three of the titles given to Jesus in the Gospel are used here.
   - Christ
   - Son of God (Son of the Blessed One)
   - Son of Man

   How important was each of these titles in causing Jesus to be sentenced? **PS 2.1, 2.3**

2  What is blasphemy? Do you think blasphemy should be treated as a crime in the twenty-first century? **PS 2.1, 2.3**

## Key points

- The trial was about Jesus' authority.
- The deciding moment came when Jesus said he was the Son of God.
- Jesus was sentenced for blasphemy.

## The Roman trial

### Jesus before Pilate

During the night Jesus had been arrested and put on trial in front of the Sanhedrin. First thing in the morning, they brought him to Pilate, the Roman governor.

> Very early in the morning, the chief priests, with the elders, the teachers of the law and the whole Sanhedrin, reached a decision. They bound Jesus, led him away and handed him over to Pilate.
> 'Are you the king of the Jews?' asked Pilate.
> 'Yes, it is as you say,' Jesus replied.
> The chief priests accused him of many things. So again Pilate asked him, 'Aren't you going to answer? See how many things they are accusing you of.'
> But Jesus still made no reply, and Pilate was amazed. (15: 1-5)

- Jesus had been condemned by the high priest for blasphemy because he said he was the Son of God. He had condemned him as worthy of death. That was all he could do. The priests did not have the authority to order a crucifixion. They took Jesus to Pilate.

- Pilate was the Roman governor of Judaea from AD 26 to AD 36. He was a cruel, harsh ruler. A letter exists from Herod Agrippa, king of Galilee, to the Roman Emperor. In his letter he writes that Pilate was 'inflexible, merciless and obstinate' and gives a list of his terrible cruelties.

- Pilate asked Jesus, 'Are you the king of the Jews?' Jesus said that he was. He was the Messiah.

- Pilate's job, as Roman governor, was to make sure there were no rebellions against the power of the Roman Emperor. He certainly did not want any Jewish kings around in Jerusalem. Even Herod, who was king in Galilee, only kept his throne because the Roman Emperor allowed him to do so.

- Pilate might well have wanted Jesus out of the way. However, even though Jesus said he was king of the Jews, Pilate obviously didn't think he was a danger.

### Jesus or Barabbas?

Now it was the custom at the Feast to release a prisoner whom the people requested. A man called Barabbas was in prison with the insurrectionists who had committed murder in the uprising. The crowd came up and asked Pilate to do for them what he usually did.

> 'Do you want me to release to you the king of the Jews?' asked Pilate, knowing it was out of envy that the chief priests had handed Jesus over to him.
> But the chief priests stirred up the crowd to have Pilate release Barabbas instead.
> 'What shall I do, then, with the one you call the king of the Jews?' Pilate asked them.
> 'Crucify him!' they shouted.
> 'Why? What crime has he committed?' asked Pilate.
> But they shouted all the louder, 'Crucify him!'
> Wanting to satisfy the crowd, Pilate released Barabbas to them. He had Jesus flogged, and handed him over to be crucified. (15: 6-15)

- A crowd came to ask that Pilate would free a prisoner. Apparently it was something that happened every year at Passover.

- An insurrection is a rebellion. Barabbas was not only a rebel but also a murderer.

- It was the chief priests who got the crowd to shout for Barabbas. They would have accepted anyone rather than Jesus.

- Pilate asked what crime Jesus had committed. Jesus had said he was the king of the Jews, but had he actually done anything wrong?

- Pilate sent Jesus to be crucified. He did this not because of what Jesus had done, but because he didn't want a riot. The Jews were a difficult nation to govern and Pilate did not want trouble.

- Not content with the terrible penalty of crucifixion, Pilate first had Jesus flogged.

## Did Pilate give Jesus a fair trial?

As Mark describes it, the trial was obviously not conducted fairly. In fact, it was not a proper trial at all.

- The trial did not take place after proper notice and preparation. A short time after Jesus was brought to Pilate, he was sentenced to death.

- Pilate seems to have thought Jesus was innocent. Even so, he gave way to pressure and sentenced him.

- In the end Pilate sentenced Jesus to flogging and death without knowing what crime he had committed.

## The mocking of Jesus by the soldiers

The soldiers led Jesus away into the palace (that is, the Praetorium) and called together the whole company of soldiers. They put a purple robe on him, then twisted together a crown of thorns and set it on him. And they began to call out to him, 'Hail, king of the Jews!' Again and again they struck him on the head with a staff and spit on him. Falling on their knees, they paid homage to him. And when they had mocked him, they took off the purple robe and put his own clothes on him. Then they led him out to crucify him. (15: 16-20)

Jesus was a condemned criminal. His offence was, apparently, to have claimed to be king of the Jews. To the soldiers the idea of Jesus as a king was a great joke. They mocked him – they made fun of him. They called all the other soldiers to join in the mockery.

- They dressed him like a king – in royal purple.
- They made him a crown – of thorns. The pain must have been excruciating.
- They greeted him mockingly – 'Hail, king of the Jews'.
- They went down on their knees in mock homage.
- At the same time, they humiliated Jesus, spitting on him and hitting him on the head.

*This spot in the Convent of the Sisters of Sion is said to be the place where Jesus was tried by Pontius Pilate.*

### Activities

1. Forum theatre: Jesus in front of Pilate. Possibilities for intervention by priests and any Romans present.
   C 2.1a, PS 2.2, 2.3, WO 2.2, 2.3

2. Describe in your own words the way in which the soldiers mocked Jesus. Why do you think they thought it was fun to do so?
   PS 2.1, 2.3

### Key points

- Pilate, the Roman governor, was concerned to maintain law and order.
- Pilate did not think Jesus had done anything wrong.
- Pilate offered the people the choice between Jesus and Barabbas. Egged on by the priests, they chose Barabbas.
- Pilate sentenced Jesus so as to avoid a riot.
- The soldiers made fun of the idea that Jesus was a king.

## Golgotha

Mark gives a straightforward, factual account of the crucifixion. He describes how Jesus was taken to Golgotha and put on the cross to die. He concentrates on what was happening to Jesus and how different people reacted to seeing Jesus being crucified. He records just one thing which Jesus said during the crucifixion.

It is important to understand that for Christians the death of Jesus has always been a crucial event. Mark was writing to describe the crucifixion for the benefit of people who needed to know exactly what happened.

Mark does not make much of the physical suffering of Jesus. Plenty of people were crucified at the time of the Roman Empire. Much more important for Mark is to show how Jesus bore the suffering, so that his readers would be helped to understand who Jesus was.

## Simon of Cyrene

> A certain man from Cyrene, Simon, the father of Alexander and Rufus, was passing by on his way in from the country, and they forced him to carry the cross. (15: 21)

It was usual for a condemned criminal to carry his own cross beam to the place of execution. However, the weight was perhaps too heavy for Jesus in his weakened state, so a bystander was apparently made to carry it for him.

Why should Mark have bothered to mention that this man carried the cross of Jesus? Why should he have named Simon – and even given the names of his sons? The natural explanation is that some people reading the Gospel might have known Alexander and Rufus. There was a Rufus among the Christians at Rome, where Mark probably wrote his Gospel.

Remember that it is important to Christians that what the Bible says is true. By naming Simon and his sons Mark stressed that the event really happened – it involved the father of someone his readers might have known.

## Jesus Crucified

> They brought Jesus to the place called Golgotha (which means The Place of the Skull). Then they offered him wine mixed with myrrh, but he did not take it. And they crucified him. Dividing up his clothes, they cast lots to see what each would get.
>
> It was the third hour when they crucified him. The written notice of the charge against him read: THE KING OF THE JEWS. They crucified two robbers with him, one on his right and one on his left. (15: 22-7)

- Jesus was offered wine mixed with myrrh to deaden the pain. He did not accept it; he endured the full agony of crucifixion.

- It was the custom for those on duty at a crucifixion to share the clothes of the person crucified.

- The crucifixion began at the third hour – about nine in the morning by our reckoning.

- The charge given was simply THE KING OF THE JEWS. There was nothing to say whether Jesus actually said he was the king of the Jews. There was no statement that Jesus was guilty of rebellion. In fact, what was written on the notice was not an accusation at all.

*The words 'King of the Jews' were written in Hebrew, Greek and Latin. The Latin words are Iesus Nazarenus Rex Iudaeorum. The initials of those four words are often seen on crucifixes.*

## The mocking continues

Those who passed by hurled insults at him, shaking their heads and saying, 'So! You who are going to destroy the temple and build it in three days, come down from the cross and save yourself!'

In the same way the chief priests and the teachers of the law mocked him among themselves. 'He saved others,' they said, 'but he can't save himself! Let this Christ, this King of Israel, come down now from the cross, that we may see and believe.' Those crucified with him also heaped insults on him. (15: 29-32)

- Insults were hurled at Jesus as he hung on the cross. He had shown great power when he performed miracles to help others. What could he do to help himself?

- At the trial before the high priest Jesus had been accused of saying 'I will destroy this man-made temple and in three days will build another, not made by man' (see pages 28–9).

- If Jesus had just stepped off the cross unharmed, that would have been an amazing miracle. Jesus did not do it.

### Activities

1  Look for other pictures of the crucifixion or for crucifixes. Think about the meaning or message behind each one. Is the meaning always the same? **PS 2.1, 2.2**

2  If Jesus had just stepped down from the cross, would this have convinced anyone that he was the Son of God? Give reasons for your answer. **PS 2.1, 2.3**

### Key points

- Jesus refused to accept anything which would have deadened or eased his suffering.

- The charge against Jesus was simply given as 'The King of the Jews'.

- During the crucifixion Jesus was mocked by the bystanders, who taunted him, telling him to use his power to come down from the cross.

# The death of Jesus

## 'My God, my God, why have you forsaken me?'

The crucifixion lasted six hours. It was a long, lingering death. Mark describes how it ended and the impression made on the Roman centurion in charge.

> At the sixth hour darkness came over the whole land until the ninth hour. And at the ninth hour Jesus cried out in a loud voice, 'Eloi, Eloi, lama sabachthani?' – which means, 'My God, my God, why have you forsaken me?'
>
> When some of those standing near heard this, they said, 'Listen, he's calling Elijah.' One man ran, filled a sponge with wine vinegar, put it on a stick, and offered it to Jesus to drink. 'Now leave him alone. Let's see if Elijah comes to take him down,' he said. (15: 33-6)

- 'The sixth hour' means midday. 'The ninth hour' means about 3 p.m.

- Mark quotes the actual Aramaic words that Jesus spoke. He had to give the Aramaic since otherwise the response about Elijah would not make sense to his readers. The four Aramaic words have a powerful dramatic force.

- Jesus was using the opening words from Psalm 22. It may be that he was using them as a prayer. This psalm contains many verses which seem to relate to the crucifixion of Jesus.

- One way in which people understand the words of Jesus is that he felt himself deserted by the Father. Jesus was bearing the punishment for sin on behalf of the human race. The punishment for sin is to be separated from God. This experience was far worse than the physical pain of the cross. Of all his sufferings, the separation from God especially was what made Jesus cry out in agony.

- Either those standing nearby didn't hear properly what Jesus said or they pretended not to hear. They made fun of Jesus by saying he must be calling on Elijah to help him. Elijah was one of the greatest of the prophets in the Old Testament.

He had been dead for over 800 years. The idea that Elijah would come to help Jesus was a great joke to the bystanders.

The prophet Malachi seemed to say that Elijah would come to prepare the way for the Messiah (Malachi 4: 5).

In his description of the Transfiguration (9: 2-13) Mark describes Jesus talking with Moses and Elijah. Christians see the Transfiguration as the Father endorsing Jesus as his Son (see pages 14–15). It seems to them ironic that at the crucifixion Jesus' enemies mocked the idea of him talking to Elijah when some weeks earlier they had been seen talking to each other.

## The death of Jesus

> With a loud cry, Jesus breathed his last. The curtain of the temple was torn in two from top to bottom. And when the centurion, who stood there in front of Jesus, heard his cry and saw how he died, he said, 'Surely this man was the Son of God!'
>
> Some women were watching from a distance. Among them were Mary Magdalene, Mary the mother of James the younger and of Joses, and Salome. In Galilee these women had followed him and cared for his needs. Many other women who had come up with him to Jerusalem were also there. (15: 37-41)

- Mark intended his readers to understand the death of Jesus as a world-shattering event. The curtain of the temple was torn in two. The curtain hung in front of the **Holy of Holies**, the most holy part of the temple, the place where above all God was believed to be present. The tearing of the temple curtain is seen by some as a sign that the way to God is open because of the death of Jesus. It is also seen as a sign that the old system of coming to the temple with an offering to God, as laid down in the Old Testament law, had come to an end.

- A centurion was a senior officer in the Roman army. He was probably the officer in charge at the crucifixion. He was not a Jew and would not have believed in God in the same way as Jews did. As far as is known, he had not come across Jesus before the crucifixion. His response to the death of Jesus, 'Surely this man was the Son of God!' is spontaneous. What did the centurion mean? Probably he meant that Jesus was a very great man, even godlike. It was a sincere tribute from a total stranger.

- Remember that the first verse of Mark's Gospel is 'The beginning of the gospel about Jesus Christ, the Son of God.' Here at the end of the description of the crucifixion – such a vital part of the Gospel – come these same words from the centurion. To him as well, Jesus was the Son of God.

## Activities

1. Look up Psalm 22. Can you find words in the psalm which seem relevant to the crucifixion of Jesus? **PS 2.1, 2.2**

2. Make a copy of the plan of the temple on page 6 and mark where the curtain of the temple would have been. Note how when it tore, the Holy of Holies, which was supposed to be hidden from the sight of all but the high priest, would have been exposed. You may find the websites on page 7 useful. **PS 2.1**

## Key points

- Mark only records one thing that Jesus said during the crucifixion – 'My God, my God, why have you forsaken me?'

- When Jesus died, the centurion in charge of the crucifixion said 'Surely this man was the Son of God'.

# Why did Jesus die?

## Key terms

**Sacrifice** An offering to God. Some sacrifices in the Bible are seen as offerings to show God that the person offering them is sorry for sins committed and wishes in some way to pay for the sin. The death of Jesus is seen by Christians as the perfect offering to God, to take away the sins of the world.

## A wonderful mystery

Christians think of the death of Jesus as a great and wonderful mystery. They do not pretend they can fully understand why Jesus was crucified. They do believe that in some marvellous way the death of Jesus can save them from the effects of their sins and give them hope of being with God in heaven after they have died.

## Jesus' enemies had him put to death

That is the obvious answer to the question, 'Why did Jesus die?' His enemies plotted against him. They arranged that one of his followers should betray him. They caught him in the garden of Gethsemane. Jesus was helpless as the soldiers seized him and his disciples ran away. He was trapped into saying that he was the Son of God. The priests persuaded Pilate to sentence him to death. He was crucified.

On one level, that is the answer. But for Christians that is only a small part of the answer. It is not what Mark intended his readers to understand.

Christians today believe Jesus died because he chose to die, in God's plan, for the sins of the world.

## Jesus knew he was going to die

Jesus told his disciples a number of times that he was going to die and rise again. The disciples did not grasp what he meant.

Each time Jesus talked about his coming death he spoke of himself as the Son of Man.

The Son of Man was the heavenly figure referred to in the Book of Daniel. Whenever Jesus used the title Son of Man it was with a sense of his own unique destiny.

For instance, 9: 31-2:

He said to them, 'The Son of Man is going to be betrayed into the hands of men. They will kill him, and after three days he will rise.' But they did not understand what he meant and were afraid to ask him about it.

## Jesus went deliberately to his death

Jesus could have avoided his arrest and death. In many ways he seemed to go deliberately towards his crucifixion.

- He went to Jerusalem, knowing what would happen when he got there. The disciples were apprehensive about going but Jesus went forward, telling the disciples about what was to come but going to Jerusalem none the less.

  The disciples still were not getting the message. This was the occasion when James and John asked Jesus for the chief places in his kingdom. 'You don't know what you are asking,' Jesus said. 'Can you drink the cup I drink or be baptized with the baptism I am baptized with?' 'We can,' they answered – but whether they understood what he was saying is doubtful (see page 17).

- Jesus rode into Jerusalem on a donkey. That was asking for trouble. By entering Jerusalem in this way he showed that he claimed to be Messiah.

- At the Last Supper Jesus knew that Judas was going to betray him – but he did not try to stop him leaving to go to the chief priests.

- Jesus knew Judas would bring the soldiers to Gethsemane – but he still went to pray there.

- Jesus did not try to prove his innocence – even though Pilate seemed to be on his side.

## The Son of Man gave his life as a ransom for many

Jesus said, 'The Son of Man did not come to be served, but to serve, and to give his life as a ransom for many.' In other words, his death in some way took away the punishment deserved by sinners because of the sins of which they were guilty.

Sin is disobeying the will of God. When people sin, they are breaking God's law. Sin separates the human race from God. By sinning, human beings set up a barrier between themselves and God.

Jesus gave his life to remove that barrier. The death of Jesus was a ransom which in a sense paid the price of sin.

## Jesus' death was a sacrifice

In the Old Testament law the people were told to offer certain **sacrifices** to God, often by killing a lamb or other animal from their flock. The **Day of Atonement** was a special day on which they were to offer special sacrifices to pray for God's forgiveness. One such offering was the scapegoat, the goat which was sent off into the wilderness bearing away the sins of the people.

The offerings in the Old Testament law had to be offered year by year. Jesus' death was the perfect sacrifice, offered to God, to reconcile the human race to him. Jesus' sacrifice was complete and never needs to be repeated.

## God so loved the world that he gave his only Son

Christians believe in God as a loving Father. It was because of God's love for the human race that Jesus was born, died and rose again. Jesus took the step which would allow people to be forgiven and to be close to God.

# What does Jesus' death mean for Christians today?

Christians believe that their relationship with God depends on the death and resurrection of Jesus. Without the death of Jesus human beings have no chance of being close to God or of obtaining forgiveness from their sins.

Christians must accept for themselves the benefits of Jesus' death. There has to be a response to the love of God. Individual Christians must accept Jesus as a personal saviour and lord.

Christians believe that through baptism they can receive the benefits of the death of Jesus. They remember the words of Paul in his letter to the Christians in Rome.

*To many people Good Friday is a holiday, a day for shopping. These Christians are trying to bring home to people that Good Friday is a holy day, a day for remembering the crucifixion of Jesus.*

> Or don't you know that all of us who were baptized into Christ Jesus were baptized into his death? We were therefore buried with him through baptism into death in order that, just as Christ was raised from the dead through the glory of the Father, we too may live a new life. (Romans 6: 3-4)

Christians who baptize by total immersion (being lowered completely into the water – see pages 110, 114 and 115) believe that the immersion symbolizes dying to sin with Christ, and the rising from the water symbolizes rising to new life with Jesus (see the spread on believers' baptism, pages 112–114).

## Activities

1 Many people wear crosses and crucifixes. Why do they do so? Is it right for people who are not Christians to wear them? **PS 2.1**

## Key points

Christians believe that:

- The death of Jesus was a sacrifice freely made by him.
- Since Jesus' life was free from sin, God's love for the human race is shown by his giving his Son to die for their sins.
- Through baptism Christians share Jesus' risen life.

# Exam questions to practise

Below are some sample exam questions on the suffering and death of Jesus. The first two have examiner's tips to give you some hints on how to score full marks. The others are for you to try on your own. A good idea is to work out your own hints on how to score full marks before answering them.

1 Two other men were crucified with Jesus.
   a) Who were the other two men on the crosses? What does Mark say about them? (2)
   b) Jesus cried out, *'Eloi, Eloi, lama sabachthani?'*
      (i) What do these words mean? (2)
      (ii) What was the reaction of the onlookers? (4)

2 a) Describe the Roman trial of Jesus. (6)
   b) Why did Pilate find it difficult to decide what to do with Jesus? (4)

Now try these questions with no hints. Before you write an answer try to write down your own hints on how to score full marks.

3 a) Describe what happened from the time Jesus reached Gethsemane to the point at which he said 'Here comes my betrayer.'(7)
   b) From what you have read in Mark's Gospel, why do you think Jesus went to Gethsemane, instead of avoiding a place where he knew there would be danger? (4)

4 Explain two ways in which the crucifixion is relevant to Christians today. (6)

## How to score full marks

1 This is a question to test what you know. It should be assessed point by point. Make sure you answer the questions fully. For instance in (a) you would get one mark for saying who the men were and a second mark for what Mark said about them. Make sure you have given two separate points. Note what Mark has written in 15: 32. In (b)(ii) the number of marks available shows that you need to give a full answer.

2 This question is testing what you know and what you understand. In (b) you need to make clear who Pilate was, what sort of person he was; you must also show you are aware of the pressure he was under from the priests and his own feelings about Jesus.

**This section includes:**

- The burial of Jesus and the empty tomb
- Resurrection appearances
- Christian beliefs about the resurrection
- Christian beliefs about life after death

This section looks at the burial of Jesus, the finding of the empty tomb and the occasions when Jesus appeared after the resurrection.

Mark's Gospel may have ended very abruptly at 16: 8; the following verses were probably added later.

Christians see the resurrection of Jesus as something quite amazing, something quite impossible by human standards. Yet they are convinced Jesus did rise from the dead. People have different ideas about what did happen to the body of Jesus. They agree that Jesus is present with them in the world of the twenty-first century. Christians believe that after death there is life with God for the followers of Jesus.

# The burial of Jesus and the empty tomb

## Jesus' body

It was **Preparation Day** (that is, the day before the Sabbath). So as evening approached, Joseph of Arimathea, a prominent member of the Council, who was himself waiting for the kingdom of God, went boldly to Pilate and asked for Jesus' body. Pilate was surprised to hear that he was already dead. Summoning the centurion, he asked him if Jesus had already died. When he learned from the centurion that it was so, he gave the body to Joseph. (15: 42-5)

- Joseph was himself a member of the Sanhedrin, the Council as it is called here. The other Gospels tell us that he was a follower of Jesus and that he had not been among those who voted to condemn Jesus. Mark shows that Joseph was a follower of Jesus by saying that Joseph was waiting for the kingdom of God.

- Joseph was important enough to be able to go straight to the governor, Pilate. He showed his support for Jesus and all that he stood for by asking for the body of Jesus, so that Jesus could be given a proper burial. If Joseph had not done this, Jesus' body would have been thrown into a large mass grave, along with the others being crucified with him.

- Time was short. The **Sabbath** is Saturday. Jesus was crucified on a Friday, the preparation day. (Christians call the day of the crucifixion of Jesus 'Good Friday'.) What is more, the Sabbath begins at sunset. Joseph and the women with him didn't have much time in which to bury Jesus, without breaking the law about not working on the Sabbath.

## The burial of Jesus

So Joseph bought some linen cloth, took down the body, wrapped it in the linen, and placed it in a tomb cut out of rock. Then he rolled a stone against the entrance of the tomb. Mary Magdalene and Mary the mother of Joses saw where he was laid. (15: 46-7)

What Joseph and the women were able to do was not a full burial. They didn't have time to complete the rite before the Sabbath began. They had to leave the work of burial until the Sabbath was over. So, on the Sabbath, the Saturday, Jesus' body was left to lie in the tomb.

The grave in which they buried Jesus was a cave cut into rock. Although they were going to return, they clearly thought that the stone was sufficient to make the tomb secure.

*The Garden Tomb in Jerusalem. Jesus would have been buried in a tomb like this.*

## The Empty Tomb

When the women came back to the grave after the Sabbath they wondered who would open the tomb for them – they did not expect to do it themselves. When they arrived at the tomb, it was empty. The body of Jesus had gone. Many Christians regard the empty tomb as proof that Jesus had risen – he had come back to life.

When the Sabbath was over, Mary Magdalene, Mary the mother of James, and Salome bought spices so that they might go to anoint Jesus' body. Very early on the first day of the week, just after sunrise, they were on their way to the tomb and they asked each other, 'Who will roll the stone away from the entrance of the tomb?'

But when they looked up, they saw that the stone, which was very large, had been rolled away. As they entered the tomb, they saw a young man dressed in a white robe sitting on the right side, and they were alarmed.

'Don't be alarmed,' he said. 'You are looking for Jesus the Nazarene, who was crucified. He has risen! He is not here. See the place where they laid him. But go, tell his disciples and Peter, "He is going ahead of you into Galilee. There you will see him, just as he told you."'

Trembling and bewildered, the women went out and fled from the tomb. They said nothing to anyone, because they were afraid. (16: 1-8)

- We are clearly meant to think that the young man is an angel, a messenger from God. The women were frightened at the sight of the angel.

- The message was amazing. 'He has risen. He is not here.'

- The young man drew the women's attention to the spot where Jesus' body had been: 'See the place where they laid him.' They had to believe the evidence of their own eyes. Jesus had gone.

- Then came something even more amazing. 'You will actually see Jesus for yourselves. Go to Galilee. You will see him there.'

- The message must have sounded impossibly strange. The tomb was empty because Jesus was alive. They themselves would see him.

## The ending to Mark's Gospel

In the most ancient copies of Mark's Gospel, the oldest Greek manuscripts, the Gospel ends at chapter 16 verse 8, as above. In other manuscripts verses 9-20 are added; in a few there is a different, shorter ending. It does seem that verse 8 is the end of the Gospel Mark wrote and that other people tried to complete it.

Why did the Gospel end here? There are two possible answers

- There should be a longer ending. Perhaps Mark died and never finished it. Perhaps the last few verses got lost.

- It is possible that Mark deliberately stopped here. The tomb was empty. The angel had told them that Jesus had risen. There was nothing else to say. The empty tomb and the words of the angel were evidence of the resurrection of Jesus Christ.

> In tears of grief, dear Lord, we leave Thee
> Hearts cry to Thee, O Saviour dear
> Lie Thou softly, softly here.
> Rest thy worn and bruised body
> At Thy grave, O Jesus blest.
> May the sinner, worn with weeping,
> Comfort find in Thy dear keeping
> And the weary soul find rest.
> Sleep in peace, sleep Thou in the Father's breast.

*The words of the final chorale of Bach's St Matthew Passion.*

### Activities

1  Listen to a recording of the final chorale of Bach's St Matthew Passion or a modern musical interpretation of the death of Jesus. Discuss what emotions it produces in you. (You may wish to interpret the music in mime or dance.) **C 2.1a, WO 2.1, 2.2**

2  Hot seat: a member of the group is the angel at the empty tomb. **C 2.1a, WO 2.2, 2.3**

### Key points

- Joseph of Arimathea was given permission to bury the body of Jesus.

- Jesus' body was placed in a tomb. There was not time to complete the burial rites before sunset and the beginning of the Sabbath.

- When the women came back on the Sunday morning the tomb was empty; the body had gone.

- An angel told them that Jesus was alive again and would meet them in Galilee.

# Resurrection appearances

## People who saw Jesus

As was said on the previous page, in many ancient manuscripts Mark's Gospel ends at chapter 16, verse 8. In other versions there is a longer ending. What follows is based on that long ending.

It is incredible that someone should rise from the dead. It is against nature and it just does not happen. The first Christians knew that – and yet they were convinced that Jesus had really risen.

One reason they were so certain that Jesus had risen was that people had seen him alive. Each of the Gospels describes Jesus appearing to some of his followers.

When Jesus rose early on the first day of the week, he appeared first to Mary Magdalene, out of whom he had driven seven demons. She went and told those who had been with him and who were mourning and weeping.

When they heard that Jesus was alive and that she had seen him, they did not believe it.

Afterward Jesus appeared in a different form to two of them while they were walking in the country. These returned and reported it to the rest; but they did not believe them either. (16: 9-13)

- Each of these events is described in more detail in another Gospel. In this Gospel there is very little detail. The important thing is that Mary Magdalene did see Jesus. Also, the couple walking into the country saw Jesus.

- It was simply unbelievable. When other people were told that Jesus had been seen, they did not believe what they heard. As more and more people did see Jesus, so others began to accept what they were saying.

## 'Preach the good news to all creation.'

Later Jesus appeared to the Eleven as they were eating; he rebuked them for their lack of faith and their stubborn refusal to believe those who had seen him after he had risen.

He said to them, 'Go into all the world and preach the good news to all creation. Whoever believes and is baptised will be saved, but whoever does not believe will be condemned. And these signs will accompany those who believe: In my name they will drive out demons; they will speak in new tongues; they will pick up snakes with their hands; and when they drink deadly poison, it will not hurt them at all; they will place their hands on sick people, and they will get well.' (16: 14-18)

- The appearance to the Eleven (the original twelve disciples except for Judas) is also described in another Gospel.

- Jesus first reprimanded them for not having believed him when he told them he would rise from the dead, even when other people told them that he had risen and that they had seen him.

- Jesus sent the disciples out to spread the gospel. They were to go to 'all creation'. Christians have always believed that they have a **mission** to tell everyone, of every nation, the gospel of Jesus. The command to go out and preach the gospel is called the Great **Commission**.

- Jesus said that people would be judged by their response to the gospel.

- Those who went in his name would have remarkable powers. They would be protected from harm. The words about picking up snakes seem to point to Paul's escape described in Acts 28: 1-6.

They would be able to heal people, casting out devils from some of them.

## The Ascension

After the Lord Jesus had spoken to them, he was taken up into heaven and he sat at the right hand of God. Then the disciples went out and preached everywhere, and the Lord worked with them and confirmed his word by the signs that accompanied it. (16: 19-20)

- Mark's Gospel ends on a confident note. He describes the **ascension** of Jesus – the occasion when he was taken up to heaven to sit at the right hand of God, the place of highest honour.
- Here at the ascension Jesus is called 'Lord' – a title which only comes at one other point in the whole Gospel (and then it was spoken by Jesus himself, when he sent the disciples to collect the donkey on which he rode into Jerusalem).
- When the disciples go out to preach, Jesus is still with them. What they say and do is in his power. This belief is very important to Christians today.

It is important to Christians that Jesus' life on earth ended as it did, with the ascension.

- Jesus had already died on the cross. The resurrection is a sign that Jesus offers to his followers life after death.
- The disciples saw Jesus for the last time when a cloud made it impossible for them to see him any longer. They took this as meaning that Jesus had returned to be with the Father in heaven.
- When Jesus, God the Son, was born in Bethlehem he took human nature and became a human being. He did not discard his human nature when he returned to the throne of God.

At the time of Jesus it was commonly believed that heaven was a place above the sky. That traditional idea does not fit what is now known about space. Some literalist and fundamentalist Christians believe in heaven as a place beyond space. The majority do not think of heaven as a physical place; they believe in heaven as a spiritual state, in the presence of God.

### Activities

1 Many Christian organizations are known as missions. Visit the website of the Mission Aviation Fellowship (www.maf.org). What do the members of that organization see as their mission? **IT 2.1, 2.2, PS 2.1, 2.2**

2 A hymn puts Christian belief about the Ascension into a few words:
> Jesus lives, adored by angels.
> Man with God is on the throne.
> Mighty Lord, in thine ascension
> We by faith behold our own.

Can you work out what you think it is saying? **PS 2.1**

3 Look at the picture above. Do you think such a traditional view of the Ascension can have any meaning in the twenty-first century? Give reasons for your opinion. **PS 2.1, 2.3**

### Key points

- Jesus was seen by a number of his followers. When they told others that he was alive, no one could believe it – until they had seen for themselves.
- Jesus sent his disciples out to spread the gospel to people of every nation. He promised that he would always be with them.
- The way in which Jesus' time on earth ended is a sign to Christians of his eternal life.

# Christian beliefs about the resurrection

## Key terms

**Eucharist** The ceremony at which Christians celebrate what Jesus said and did at the Last Supper. They believe that at the Eucharist the risen Jesus is with them.

## The event without which there would be no gospel

The idea that Jesus died and then was alive once more is stated clearly in the Gospels and in other books of the New Testament. Paul in his letters makes it clear that Jesus did rise from the dead. In his first letter to the Corinthians he gives a list of people who saw Jesus. The death, burial and resurrection of Jesus were the great events on which the whole Christian gospel was based.

For some people it seems that belief in the resurrection has no place in the modern world. People do not rise from the dead. It cannot happen. If it cannot happen, then it didn't happen.

It is important to remember that this is nothing new. Belief that Jesus rose from the dead has always been a problem for many people. Even in the New Testament there are plenty of examples of people who found the whole idea of the resurrection simply incredible. Note how even the disciples did not believe it at first (see page 42).

## No compromise – the resurrection really happened

From the start the resurrection was central to Christianity. The first Christians preached that Jesus had risen. They refused to give way and say it was not true – they were totally convinced. Paul was a case in point.

In Acts 26 Paul speaks to King Agrippa and the Roman governor, Festus. He tells how he became a Christian and they listen with interest. Paul finishes by saying, 'I am saying nothing beyond what the prophets and Moses said would happen – that the Christ would suffer and, as the first to rise from the dead, would proclaim light to his own people and to the Gentiles.' At this point Festus interrupted Paul.

'You are out of your mind, Paul!' he shouted. 'Your great learning is driving you insane.'

Paul did not apologize or say something like 'I didn't mean really risen'. In reply he stated firmly once again his belief that Jesus had risen from the dead.

Many Christians believe as Paul did that Jesus did physically rise from the dead. They also believe that after the resurrection the body of Jesus was in some way different. People who knew Jesus well did not recognize him at first, according to Luke and John. Paul talks about a physical body and a spiritual body.

## The resurrection body of Jesus

For all Christians the important thing about the resurrection of Jesus is that he is alive now. Death did not destroy him. He was a living spiritual reality to his followers even after he was crucified. They experienced his power and presence with them. In the same way Christians today experience Jesus as a living spiritual power, present with them in their everyday lives.

Different Christians have different views about what happened to the body of Jesus after the resurrection. To many Christians, the body of the risen Jesus was the same body as before. The wounds from the crucifixion were there in his hands, feet and side. But the body had been transformed. Jesus was able to come and go even when doors were shut. For instance, in John 20: 19 it reads 'On the evening of that first day of the week, when the disciples were together, with the doors locked for fear of the Jews, Jesus came and stood among them and said, "Peace be with you!"' Yet Jesus was not a ghost. He told his disciples to touch him and be sure that he was really there.'

## Another way of understanding the resurrection of Jesus

Some Christians do not attach much importance to the physical aspect of the resurrection. They may find it difficult to cope with the idea. To them, the important aspect of the resurrection of Jesus is that he is alive and present with people today.

Christians holding such beliefs are sometimes accused of not believing that Jesus rose from the dead. Their attitude is that it does not matter whether the tomb was empty or whether Jesus returned to earth in a bodily form. If people find it difficult to believe in that sort of resurrection, there is no need for them to pretend to believe what they do not believe. What matters is that Jesus was and is really present. A person who believes that the risen Jesus is alive in the world today can be a true Christian.

## 'I am with you always'

The last words Jesus spoke in Matthew's Gospel are 'I am with you always, to the very end of the age'. The resurrection shows that Jesus is the Son of God. Christians rely on his promise that he will always be with them.

- Christians feel they can pray to God at any time. They believe Jesus is with them and that his death and resurrection make it possible for them to speak to God. They often pray '…through Jesus Christ, our Lord'.

- They believe that Jesus is truly present with them in the **Eucharist**. He is with them in his risen power. Many Christians believe that the bread and wine are the body and blood of Christ. It is the risen Jesus who is with them. See the pages on the Eucharist (pages 98–103).

- Christians believe that wherever they are or whatever they do Jesus is with them.

*Many Christians see a cross without a figure of Christ on it as showing that Jesus has risen from death.*

*This Orthodox crucifix shows the risen Jesus, the great High Priest in heaven.*

## Activities

1 Look at Acts 2 and read the speech made by Peter on the Day of Pentecost, just seven weeks after the resurrection. Write down what he said about the crucifixion and resurrection. What proportion of his speech is about the death and resurrection of Jesus and what it means? **PS 2.1, 2.3**

2 Easter eggs are popular symbols of the resurrection. Why is this so? (Remember – think of real eggs, not chocolate eggs!)
**PS 2.1**

## Key points

- Belief in the resurrection of Jesus is of the highest importance to Christians today.
- Some Christians believe that the body of Jesus actually rose, physically. Others say that that sort of resurrection is difficult to accept – or doesn't matter anyway.
- Christians believe that the risen Jesus is always with them, as he promised he would be.

# Christian beliefs about life after death

## What Jesus taught

Jesus taught that there is life after death. In Mark's Gospel there are a number of places where he refers to that belief. The place where the teaching of Jesus is clearest is in the account of his confrontation with members of one of the religious groups, the Sadducees.

### Jesus and the Sadducees

The Sadducees did not believe that the soul could survive death. When the body died that was it. When Jesus was teaching in the temple at Jerusalem a few days before his crucifixion, they tackled him on the matter.

On the face of it, the Sadducees were asking a question about a particular family situation. In reality, they were making fun of the whole idea of life after death.

> Then the Sadducees, who say there is no resurrection, came to him with a question.
>
> 'Teacher,' they said, 'Moses wrote for us that if a man's brother dies and leaves a wife but no children, the man must marry the widow and have children for his brother. Now there were seven brothers. The first one married and died without leaving any children. The second one married the widow, but he also died, leaving no child. It was the same with the third. In fact, none of the seven left any children. Last of all, the woman died too. At the resurrection whose wife will she be, since the seven were married to her?'
>
> Jesus replied, 'Are you not in error because you do not know the Scriptures or the power of God? When the dead rise, they will neither marry nor be given in marriage; they will be like the angels in heaven. Now about the dead rising – have you not read in the book of Moses, in the account of the bush, how God said to him, "I am the God of Abraham, the God of Isaac, and the God of Jacob"? He is not the God of the dead, but of the living. You are badly mistaken!' (12: 18-27)

This passage needs to be studied carefully. Remember that it is about the key issue – can there be life after death?

- The Sadducees kept the law of Moses. They regarded the first five books of the scriptures, which contained the law, as the most holy and important part of the scriptures. The law of Moses was a word from God. Jesus couldn't just say the law was wrong.

- The Sadducees quoted the law. If a man dies, his brother must marry the widow. There is the law – no arguing.

- So, the Sadducees went on, what if all seven brothers in turn marry her? She dies last. When the dead rise, whose wife is she? They meant – what a nonsense this life after death is.

- Jesus challenged them directly. 'You do not know the scriptures.' That would have hurt! The Sadducees would reckon that no one knew the law as well as they did. They devoted their lives to studying it, poring over its meaning.

- Jesus went on to say that life after death will not be like that. People will be like the angels in heaven. He explained no further. He had another point to make.

- Jesus went back to the law of Moses. He reminded them of the time when God spoke to Moses from a bush that was on fire but not burning away. (You can read about Moses at the burning bush in the Old Testament, Exodus chapter 3.) God said, 'I am the God of Abraham, the God of Isaac, and the God of Jacob'. Abraham, Isaac and Jacob had all been dead for centuries. God is not the God of people who do not exist, said Jesus. Abraham, Isaac and Jacob are alive. They still exist because there is life after death.

### Other places where Jesus mentions life after death

**9: 43, 45.** Jesus makes clear that there will be a judgement and that some people will go to hell.

'If your hand causes you to sin, cut it off. It is better for you to enter life maimed than with two hands to go into hell, where the fire never goes out.'

**10: 28-31.** Jesus tells Peter and his other followers that those who leave things that are dear to them for his sake will receive rewards in this age 'and in the age to come, eternal life'.

**10: 35-45.** James and John ask Jesus for the chief places in his glory. Jesus told them that those places were not his to give. Jesus was thinking of glory as being with the Father.

**14: 25.** When Jesus gave the cup to the disciples, he told them, 'I will not drink again of the fruit of the vine until that day when I drink it anew in the kingdom of God.'

Jesus makes it clear that there is life after death. For his followers, that life will be with him and with God the Father, in the kingdom of God.

There is very little in Mark's Gospel about what life after death will be like. Elsewhere in the New Testament it is clear that the followers of Jesus believed that it would be more real and more wonderful than life here and now.

A belief in life after death is very important to Christians. It is this belief which makes the Christian faith relevant to people today.

- It helps them to make sense of the fact that in many ways life seems unfair. People sometimes ask why life is easy for some people while others have to face great suffering. Much human suffering is caused by other human beings. Jesus did not promise that there would be no suffering for his followers. He himself suffered unjustly through the actions of other people. Jesus promised his followers peace and happiness in the life which follows death.

- It gives them support when they are bereaved. Christians believe that, because death is not the end, they can entrust their loved ones to the love and mercy of God.

- It gives them an extra purpose in living. Christians believe that one day they will be judged, like everyone else. Even though they have done wrong in their lives, they believe that, because Jesus died to save them, their sins can be forgiven. Jesus has promised that those who love and serve him will be welcomed into the kingdom of God.

*What Christian beliefs are represented on this tombstone?*

Christians do not believe in reincarnation. Reincarnation means that a person returns to earth and lives again as somebody or something else. This is not a Christian belief and you will lose marks if you say that Christians do believe in reincarnation.

### Activities

1  Look at obituary notices in the paper or inscriptions on tombstones. Do the words show any belief in life after death? If so, what beliefs are there? Would you say they are Christian beliefs? **PS 2.1**

2  Look at one or two hymns which are often sung at funerals. Examples are 'Abide with me', 'The Lord's my Shepherd' and 'The Old Rugged Cross'. Why do people choose hymns like these? **PS 2.1**

### Key points

- Jesus taught that there is life after death.
- Because Jesus died to take away sin, that life will be with God for those who accept Jesus as their Saviour.
- Belief in a life with God after death, both for oneself and for one's loved ones, makes the Christian faith relevant to people today.

# Exam questions to practise

Below are some sample exam questions on resurrection and life after death. The first two have examiner's tips to give you some hints on how to score full marks. The others are for you to try on your own. A good idea is to work out your own hints on how to score full marks before answering them.

1   Describe what happened when the women went on the Sunday to the tomb. (6)

2   Look at the drawing of a headstone on page 47. Do you think the stone shows a Christian belief in life after death? Give reasons for your answer, showing you have considered more than one point of view. (5)

Now try these questions with no hints. Before you write an answer try to write down your own hints on how to score full marks.

3   What did Jesus say to the eleven disciples when he met them after the resurrection? (4)

4   Why is the resurrection of Jesus important to Christians today? (6)

## How to score full marks

1   This is a question to test what you know. It would be marked on a point-by-point basis. For full marks, virtually every significant point would need to be covered, though it would be unreasonable to expect minor details – for instance, you would not be expected to record the names of each of the women in full, as given in the text. Check the text carefully to make sure your answer is complete.

2   This is an evaluation question, testing your judgement. Make sure you look at every part of the design. You need not comment on the names, dates and ages, obviously. You should think about the words and the other parts of the design – do the flowers mean anything? Is anything missing? For instance, is there any sign of Jesus as Saviour?

# The kingdom of God

**This section includes:**

- What is the kingdom of God?
- The parable of the sower
- Other parables of the kingdom
- The kingdom of God in action

This section looks at the concept of the kingdom of God. The kingdom is where God is accepted as king. The kingdom is in the hearts of people who follow Jesus. The kingdom is also in heaven, in the presence of the Father. Christians must be prepared to make sacrifices in order to enter the kingdom.

Jesus taught about the kingdom in a series of parables. He also taught that the basis of the Christian life is love. The two great commandments are that one should love God and love one's neighbour. Anyone who kept those commandments was not far from the kingdom of God.

# What is the kingdom of God?

## 'The kingdom of God'

One of the key features in Jesus' teaching is the **kingdom of God**. He spoke about the kingdom from the very start of his ministry.

> After John was put in prison, Jesus went into Galilee, proclaiming the good news of God. 'The time has come,' he said. 'The kingdom of God is near. Repent and believe the good news!' (1: 14-15)

The kingdom of God is where God is king. It is found in the hearts of human beings. Wherever someone accepts the gospel, God is king. Accepting God is king means:

- honouring and trusting God
- obeying and serving God.

The kingdom of God is not like a human kingdom, such as the United Kingdom.

- The kingdom is not a place, in the way that the United Kingdom is a place.
- usually citizenship of the United Kingdom depends on being born or living in the United Kingdom. For most people it is something which involves no choice on their part. Membership of the kingdom of God depends on a response to the gospel. It is not automatic.

It is clear from the Gospels that Jesus thought of the kingdom in two different situations:

- in the world the kingdom is made up of people who accept God as king
- after death and judgement, God welcomes those who love him into the kingdom.

## 'Be like little children'

Being a member of God's kingdom means trusting God completely. Jesus used the example of the trusting way in which children respond to love.

> People were bringing little children to Jesus to have him touch them, but the disciples rebuked them. When Jesus saw this, he was indignant. He said to them, 'Let the little children come to me, and do not hinder them, for the kingdom of God belongs to such as these. I tell you the truth, anyone who will not receive the kingdom of God like a little child will never enter it.' And he took the children in his arms, put his hands on them and blessed them. (10: 13-16)

## 'What must I do?'

Mark describes a conversation Jesus had with a man who asked what he had to do to inherit eternal life:

> As Jesus started on his way, a man ran up to him and fell on his knees before him. 'Good teacher,' he asked, 'what must I do to inherit eternal life?'
>
> 'Why do you call me good?' Jesus answered. 'No one is good – except God alone. You know the commandments: "Do not murder, do not commit adultery, do not steal, do not give false testimony, do not defraud, honour your father and mother."'
>
> 'Teacher,' he declared, 'all these I have kept since I was a boy.'
>
> Jesus looked at him and loved him. 'One thing you lack,' he said. 'Go, sell everything you have and give to the poor, and you will have treasure in heaven. Then come, follow me.'
>
> At this the man's face fell. He went away sad, because he had great wealth. (10: 17-22)

- The man who came to Jesus genuinely wanted to gain eternal life. He was an honest, sincere person.
- Presumably the man was being polite when he called Jesus 'Good teacher'. Jesus makes him think about the meaning of the word 'good'.

- Jesus reminded him of the commandments, the central points in the law of God. The man said he had kept them since he was young.

- Jesus saw he was genuine. Jesus loved him. But there was something which was too important in the man's life – his wealth. Jesus said he must give it up.

- The man went away. He was sad at having to leave Jesus – but giving up his possessions was a sacrifice which he could not bear to make.

## 'How hard it is to enter the kingdom!'

Jesus looked around and said to his disciples, 'How hard it is for the rich to enter the kingdom of God!'

The disciples were amazed at his words. But Jesus said again, 'Children, how hard it is to enter the kingdom of God! It is easier for a camel to go through the eye of a needle than for a rich man to enter the kingdom of God.'

The disciples were even more amazed, and said to each other, 'Who then can be saved?'

Jesus looked at them and said, 'With man this is impossible, but not with God; all things are possible with God.'

Peter said to him, 'We have left everything to follow you!' 'I tell you the truth,' Jesus replied, 'no one who has left home or brothers or sisters or mother or father or children or fields for me and the gospel will fail to receive a hundred times as much in this present age (homes, brothers, sisters, mothers, children and fields – and with them, persecutions) and in the age to come, eternal life. But many who are first will be last, and the last first.' (10: 23-31)

- Jesus insisted that it is hard for someone who is rich to enter the kingdom. He uses a striking image. Clearly no camel could ever get through the eye of a needle.

- The disciples were amazed. 'Who can be saved?' Jesus reminded them that he was talking in human terms. All things are possible with God.

- When Peter said that he and the other disciples had left everything for Jesus, Jesus replied that those who gave up everything to follow him would receive a reward in this life –

but would face suffering as well. Jesus said they would also receive 'in the age to come, eternal life'.

- Jesus ended with another saying to remind his followers that God's standards are not human standards. 'Many who are first will be last, and the last first.'

*What might ownership of this car say about a person?*

## Activities

1 Look at some adverts in magazines or on TV. What do the adverts suggest the most important things in life are? What are the most important things in life? **PS 2.1**

2 Forum theatre: Jesus said 'Give to the poor'. A recent government statement said 'Do not give to beggars'. One student takes the part of a beggar. Two others walk past. **C 2.1a, PS 2.2, 2.3, WO 2.2, 2.3**

## Key points

- The kingdom of God is where God is king.
- In this life, the kingdom is found in the hearts of human beings.
- A person must be ready to sacrifice other things for the sake of the kingdom.
- After death, God welcomes those who love and serve him into the kingdom.

# The parable of the sower

Jesus told a **parable** which was, apparently, a simple description of someone sowing seed by hand. It would have been a familiar sight to his audience.

## The parable

Again Jesus began to teach by the lake. The crowd that gathered around him was so large that he got into a boat and sat in it out on the lake, while all the people were along the shore at the water's edge. He taught them many things by parables, and in his teaching said:

'Listen! A farmer went out to sow his seed. As he was scattering the seed, some fell along the path, and the birds came and ate it up. Some fell on rocky places, where it did not have much soil. It sprang up quickly, because the soil was shallow. But when the sun came up, the plants were scorched, and they withered because they had no root. Other seed fell among thorns, which grew up and choked the plants, so that they did not bear grain. Still other seed fell on good soil. It came up, grew and produced a crop, multiplying thirty, sixty, or even a hundred times.'

Then Jesus said, 'He who has ears to hear, let him hear.' (4: 1-9)

### What did Jesus mean?

Jesus told the parable and left it at that. He left people wondering, 'What is he getting at? He is not just telling us a simple story for no reason at all. There must be a hidden meaning.' They realized that he wanted them to think about what he had said and puzzle out what he meant.

Jesus ended the parable with a strange saying. 'He who has ears to hear, let him hear.' Jesus often said something like that when he wanted people to realize that what he said had a hidden meaning.

He was using the word 'hear' in two different senses. 'If anyone has ears to hear (i.e., make out what I am saying), let him hear (i.e., get the message).'

When the crowds had gone, the disciples asked for an explanation.

### The disciples want an explanation

When he was alone, the Twelve and the others around him asked him about the parables. He told them, 'The secret of the kingdom of God has been given to you. But to those on the outside everything is said in parables so that, "they may be ever seeing but never perceiving, and ever hearing but never understanding; otherwise they might turn and be forgiven!"' (4: 10-12)

### The kingdom of God

The kingdom of God – that was the key to what Jesus had been saying. The disciples knew that the kingdom was a very important part of Jesus' teaching. People who did not understand that the Parable of the Sower was about the kingdom would not be able to make any sense of it. They would, as Jesus said, hear but not understand.

It seems strange that Jesus should say, 'otherwise they might turn and be forgiven!' Obviously Jesus wanted people to repent and have their sins forgiven. The reason is that he was quoting from the Book of Isaiah in the Old Testament.

Jesus gave the disciples the explanation they wanted.

### Jesus explains

Then Jesus said to them, 'Don't you understand this parable? How then will you understand any parable? The farmer sows the word. Some people are like seed along the path, where the word is sown. As soon as they hear it, Satan comes and takes away the word that was sown in them. Others, like seed sown on rocky places, hear the word and at once receive it with joy. But since they have no root, they last only a short time. When trouble or persecution comes because of the word, they quickly fall away. Still others, like seed sown among thorns, hear the word; but the worries of this life, the deceitfulness of wealth and the desires for other things come in and choke the word, making it unfruitful. Others, like seed sown on good soil, hear the word, accept it, and produce a crop – thirty, sixty or even a hundred times what was sown.' (4: 13-20)

## The message of the parable

- The seed represents the gospel, the good news of the kingdom of God.

- Jesus does not say who the sower is. The sower is simply someone spreading the gospel.

- The places where the seed lands represent the different ways in which people respond to the gospel.

| Where seed fell | What that place meant |
|---|---|
| The path | People who hear the gospel but do not respond at all. The gospel makes no impact on them. |
| On rocky places | People who are very excited about the gospel when they first hear it. They are full of enthusiasm but the novelty wears off and they lose interest. |
| Among thorns | People who hear the gospel, but who are so absorbed with all sorts of everyday problems and interests that they do not find the time or the motivation to take the gospel seriously. |
| Good ground | People who hear the gospel and respond to it. The gospel becomes one of the most important things in their lives. They in turn pass the gospel on to other people. |

Why should I bother?

I'd love to – but I've had a row with my girlfriend.

We need collectors for Christian Aid week.

I'll help – and I'll bring some friends as well.

Love too – hang on, I'd miss Coronation Street.

## A modern version?

Imagine Jesus telling a parable today. His parable would have the same teaching. Some people simply ignore the gospel when they hear it. Others respond in the different ways shown in the original parable.

But Jesus wouldn't tell a parable about a sower. You just don't see farmers sowing seed by hand. They use a seed drill – and every seed goes where it is supposed to go. The parable would not be true to modern life. Jesus would use a different example.

### Activities

1  If Jesus were telling the parable to young people today he would take an example from their everyday life. Can you think of a good modern example? Write your parable out in the way Jesus might have told it.
**PS 2.2, 2.3**

2  An important theme of the parable is commitment. What is commitment? Is it important? **PS 2.1**

### Key points

- The idea of the kingdom of God is the key to much of Jesus' teaching.

- Different people respond to the kingdom in different ways.

When Jesus told the parable of the sower he intended to make people think through what he meant. He went on to use more parables in the same way.

## The lamp under the bowl or bed

He said to them, 'Do you bring in a lamp to put it under a bowl or a bed? Instead, don't you put it on its stand? For whatever is hidden is meant to be disclosed, and whatever is concealed is meant to be brought out into the open. If anyone has ears to hear, let him hear.'

'Consider carefully what you hear,' he continued. 'With the measure you use, it will be measured to you – and even more. Whoever has will be given more; whoever does not have, even what he has will be taken from him.' (4: 21-5)

### What Jesus meant

- Of course no one would light a lamp and then hide it. That would be useless. (It might also be dangerous, since it would have had a flame – but that is not the point Jesus was making.) A lamp is there to give light. You put the lamp where it will give light most effectively.

- Jesus continued with words which he intended his hearers to work out for themselves. 'Whatever is hidden is meant to be disclosed.' 'Whatever is concealed is meant to be brought out into the open.'

- He told them they must work out for themselves the meaning of what he was saying.

Jesus was talking about the kingdom of God. The light is the gospel of the kingdom. It must be made widely known.

*Jesus said the message of the kingdom should not be hidden.*

Jesus went on to tell two more parables about the kingdom.

## The seed growing secretly

Jesus said, 'This is what the kingdom of God is like. A man scatters seed on the ground. Night and day, whether he sleeps or gets up, the seed sprouts and grows, though he does not know how. All by itself the soil produces corn – first the stalk, then the ear, then the full grain in the ear. As soon as the grain is ripe, he puts the sickle to it, because the harvest has come.' (4: 26-9)

- The parable is simple enough. A man sows seed. He leaves it to grow. In due time he harvests what he has sown.

- In one way the man represents Jesus. In another way, the man represents those of Jesus' followers who preach the gospel.

- Certainly many preachers and teachers have no idea how people respond to what they say. People may remember what was said years later and it may change their lives – and the person who spoke the words will never know.

- Jesus himself, the Son of God, will be there at the harvest, the last judgement at the end of the world. Where he finds the seed of the gospel growing, he will bring people into the kingdom.

*A sickle.*

## The mustard seed

Again he said, 'What shall we say the kingdom of God is like, or what parable shall we use to describe it? It is like a mustard seed, which is the smallest seed you plant in the ground. Yet when planted, it grows and becomes the largest of all garden plants, with such big branches that the birds of the air can perch in its shade.' (4: 30-2)

- Jesus is talking about the kingdom on earth.
- When the kingdom began on earth, it was as small as it could be – one person, Jesus himself. (There was a saying in Palestine that the mustard seed was the smallest seed of all – though in fact it is not.)
- The kingdom has spread to every part of the world, going beyond boundaries of nationality and race and open to everyone.
- When Jesus spoke of the birds perching in the shade of the tree he might have had in mind words from the Old Testament, like those from the prophet Daniel.

The tree you saw, which grew large and strong, with its top touching the sky, ... having nesting places in its branches for the birds of the air – you, O king, are that tree! You have become great and strong ... and your dominion extends to distant parts of the earth. (Daniel 4: 20-2)

## Jesus explained the parables

With many similar parables Jesus spoke the word to them, as much as they could understand. He did not say anything to them without using a parable. But when he was alone with his own disciples, he explained everything. (4: 33-4)

Remember the conversation between Jesus and the disciples when they asked him about the meaning of the parable of the sower. These parables are a mystery, unless people realize that they are about the kingdom of God.

### Activities

1  Choose an idea which you believe to be both true and important – an example might be that everybody needs friends on whom they can rely. Write a parable which makes that point. If you prefer, instead of writing a parable, present it as a cartoon strip. **PS 2.1, 2.2**

2  Read again the parable of the lamp under the bowl or bed. Why is light a popular Christian symbol? Make a list of examples of light being used as a symbol by Christians. **PS 2.1, 2.3**

### Key points

Jesus used parables to teach about the kingdom of God.

- The lamp under a bowl teaches that the gospel of the kingdom must be made known.
- The seed growing secretly teaches that the kingdom grows, sometimes unnoticed.
- The mustard seed teaches that from a tiny beginning the kingdom grows to be vast and open to all.

# The kingdom of God in action

**Key terms**

**Church** (1) When spelt with a capital C, **Church** means Christian people. In particular, it means all Christian people. (2) When spelt with a small c, **church** means a building, a Christian place of worship.

## The two great commandments

During the week before he was crucified, Jesus spent a lot of time in the temple. While he was there many people came to ask him questions. Some were to catch him out, but this one was genuine.

> One of the teachers of the law came and heard them debating. Noticing that Jesus had given them a good answer, he asked him, 'Of all the commandments, which is the most important?'
>
> 'The most important one,' answered Jesus, 'is this: "Hear, O Israel, the Lord our God, the Lord is one. Love the Lord your God with all your heart and with all your soul and with all your mind and with all your strength." The second is this: "Love your neighbour as yourself." There is no commandment greater than these.'
>
> 'Well said, teacher,' the man replied. 'You are right in saying that God is one and there is no other but him. To love him with all your heart, with all your understanding and with all your strength, and to love your neighbour as yourself is more important than all burnt offerings and sacrifices.'
>
> When Jesus saw that he had answered wisely, he said to him, 'You are not far from the kingdom of God.' And from then on no one dared ask him any more questions. (12: 28-34)

- The commandments were the central points of the law of the Old Testament. When the rich man came to Jesus and asked what he had to do to inherit eternal life, Jesus told him he must keep the commandments (see pages 50–1).

- In fact, the two commandments Jesus chose are not among the Ten Commandments. The Ten Commandments say what people should or should not do. The commandments chosen by Jesus are of a different kind.

- The two commandments chosen by Jesus are about love – love of God and love of your neighbour. If you genuinely love anyone, you will willingly do what is necessary to please that person. If you love God, you will want to do what is right. No other commandments are needed.

- Jesus told the man that he was not far from the kingdom of God. The man had come near to the kingdom because he recognized that these commandments are the ones on which people should base their lives.

Jesus taught that the kingdom of God is in the hearts of people who accept God as king. Christians believe that the kingdom is to be found in the modern world in the hearts of people doing ordinary jobs and living ordinary lives. These people serve God in their work and in the way they treat other people.

## A modern example of loving one's neighbour

Ara was born in Syria, of Armenian parents. He has lived and worked in England since 1984. He is an Orthopaedic Surgeon in an NHS hospital. Ara is a Christian, a member of the Armenian Apostolic Church. His Christian belief influences his approach to life.

Ara says, 'To me the heart of Christianity is in the New Testament, the teachings of Jesus. Jesus taught that you should love God and love your neighbour. Jesus said "Do to others what you would have them do to you".'

As a surgeon, Ara believes that every human being matters. Each is an individual person with hopes and worries. He must not only operate on his patients but see each as a whole person. 'It is important to follow up and see what is happening to them after the operation. It is important to know how they are coping. It is important to be concerned.'

Ara was brought up believing in the need to help others. 'At Easter time my mother used to make hundreds of Easter cakes for the elderly people's home.' He believes that in most people there is a need to be charitable, to help people in need. 'All human beings have needs which must be satisfied. Just as we need to be fed, housed, clothed, so we need to be charitable. If I approach even a stranger to help me to help others – it happens! It is unbelievable!'

## Help for Armenia

Ara gives much time and effort to help people in Armenia. Armenia is a country where multiple problems followed each other, e.g. troubles left over from the Soviet regime, the massive earthquake in 1988 and the blockade of the borders from the East as well as from the West of the country. For this reason, people in Armenia are in need of many things which people in the United Kingdom can take for granted. With the help of friends, neighbours, colleagues and others, Ara and his wife, Shoghig, send supplies to places where they are needed. Supplies are sent to a base near Cirencester, from where consignments are sent to Armenia. Each year a hospital is selected. Some of the supplies are surplus to requirements in Britain because more modern equipment is now available – but what is no longer used in Britain can still be very useful in Armenia. They send anything which will be of use to people in Armenia.

Ara believes the duty to 'love your neighbour' extends to people you know and people you will never meet. As soon as individuals are self-supporting, they have the duty to start helping others. This gives feelings of satisfaction and pleasure to the giver and the receiver.

Ara.

Aid arriving in Armenia.

### Activities

1 Jesus said the two great commandments are that one should love God and one's neighbour. When he said that, what did he mean by 'love'? **PS 2.1**

2 Think about Christian people whom you know. If possible, talk to them about what they believe. How do their beliefs affect the way they live? Give a short talk to the class on what you have found. **C 2.1b, PS 2.3**

### Key points

- Jesus said the two great commandments are 'Love God and love your neighbour'.
- Jesus told the teacher of the law who agreed with him that he was not far from the kingdom of God.

# Exam questions to practise

Below are some sample exam questions on the kingdom of God. The first two have examiner's tips to give you some hints on how to score full marks. The others are for you to try on your own. A good idea is to work out your own hints on how to score full marks before answering them.

1 Give an account of the parable of the mustard seed and say what it means. (6)

2 **(a)** What did Jesus say were the two great commandments? (3)

   **(b)** 'Jesus' two great commandments are all one needs to live a good life.' Do you agree? Give reasons for your answer, showing you have considered more than one point of view. (5)

Now try these questions with no hints. Before you write an answer try to write down your own hints on how to score full marks.

3 **(a)** Tell the parable of the sower in your own words. (5)

   **(b)** 'The secret of the kingdom of God has been given to you. But to those on the outside everything is said in parables' (4: 10). What did Jesus say next? What did he mean? How did he explain the parable of the sower? (8)

4 **(a)** Give two occasions from Mark's Gospel when Jesus taught about the kingdom of God. (6)

   **(b)** What did Jesus mean by 'the kingdom of God'? (5)

## How to score full marks

1 This is a question to test what you know about the parable and whether you understand it. Make sure you give a full account of what is a very short parable and explain the meaning in as much depth as you can.

2 Note that (a) is marked out of three, indicating that more than two short points are required. (b) is an evaluation question and you should be careful to consider more than one approach.

# Faith and prayer

**This section includes:**

- Prayer
- The power of faith
- Two miracles of healing
- The meaning of the miracles
- Healing in the modern church

Jesus made a point of making time to pray and Christians follow his example. Prayer is based on faith and the search for faith. The miracles of Jesus must have seemed to many people the most striking part of his ministry. Jesus performed miracles in response to the faith of those who came to him. Some people are convinced that the power of God is shown in miraculous events today.

# Prayer

## Why did Jesus perform miracles?

One of the most attention-grabbing aspects of Jesus' ministry was his reputation as someone who could perform **miracles**. From the start of his ministry, when he healed the man with an evil spirit (1: 21-8), the miracles made people take notice of what he said and did.

Jesus did not perform miracles simply to show what remarkable things he could do. The miracles were signs of his care and love for those who suffered or were in trouble.

For miracles to take place two things were necessary – faith and prayer.

- There had to be faith on the part of the person seeking a miracle.

- Jesus himself maintained a strong bond with God the Father. He turned to the Father at many stages in his ministry, communicating with the Father through prayer.

## Jesus prayed

One occasion when Mark says that Jesus prayed was just after he had fed 5000 people. Everyone might well have wanted to see him, talk to him. But Jesus needed time for prayer.

> Immediately Jesus made his disciples get into the boat and go on ahead of him to Bethsaida, while he dismissed the crowd. After leaving them, he went up on a mountainside to pray. (6: 45-6)

Mark tells us that Jesus prayed at other difficult and challenging points of his ministry.

**1: 32-8:** Jesus had just healed a large number of sick people. Naturally, everyone wanted to see him.

Instead, he went to a quiet deserted place to pray. His disciples came to find him. They told him, 'Everyone is looking for you!' To Jesus, even when lots of people were clamouring to see him, time with the Father was essential.

**14: 35-6:** Jesus prayed at a time when he knew that he would soon be arrested, beaten and crucified. After the Last Supper he went to Gethsemane to pray. He prayed that he might not have to suffer. Then he said, 'Yet not what I will, but what you will.'

## What is prayer?

For Christians, **prayer** is communicating with God. That means, prayer is talking to God – and sometimes listening to God.

Sometimes Christians pray in the company of others. Sometimes they pray, more personally, on their own.

Christians believe firmly in the power of prayer. They believe that God is a loving Father who wishes to help and support his children. They believe that he answers prayer.

### Different aspects of prayer

Asking God for help is an important part of prayer. But Christian prayer is more than asking for things. It includes:

| | |
|---|---|
| Adoration: | God should be praised and honoured. <br> e.g. 'O God, how great you are.' |
| Thanksgiving: | Christians believe that they should thank God for everything he has given them. <br> e.g. 'We thank you, Lord, for all the good things you have given us.' |
| Confession: | Christians believe that when they have let God down in some way they should repent – admit what they have done, say they are sorry, ask to be forgiven and promise not to do the same again. <br> e.g. 'I have sinned, Lord; forgive me.' |

Intercession:   Prayer for another person or a situation that requires God's loving help and power.
e.g. 'Lord, bless and help my granddad who is ill.'

Petition:   Prayer for oneself.
e.g. 'Lord, please help me to be kind to other people.'

In any relationship, it is important to talk often if that relationship is to remain strong and meaningful. Christians think of themselves as a family, God's family. It is important that the family talks to the Father.

Christians love God and wish to share their lives with him. They need him and so they pray to him.

The link between miracle, faith and prayer is shown very strongly in the account of the healing of the epileptic boy.

### The healing of the epileptic boy

On this occasion, since Jesus was not there, the disciples had tried to heal the boy and had failed. Jesus then healed the boy.

Later his disciples asked him why they had failed. Jesus answered, 'Only prayer can drive this kind out, nothing else can.'

Jesus didn't simply mean 'You must use a good prayer; you must ask God properly'. Jesus was talking about prayer in a deeper way. He meant that his disciples must be regular in prayer and through prayer must come to a close relationship with God.

My Mum is ill, father. Please say a prayer for her.

*Here are two people at prayer. Are they praying in the same way?*

### Activities

1. Look at the drawing of the girl talking to the priest. What does the girl think prayer means? What should the priest say in reply? **PS 2.1**

2. Why did Jesus think it was important to pray? Why did he go to a quiet, deserted place? **PS 2.1**

3. Read these other examples from Mark's Gospel of times when Jesus prayed – 6: 41, 15: 34. Write down why you think Jesus prayed on these occasions. **PS 2.1, 2.3**

### Key points

- Prayer is talking with God.
- Prayer was very important to Jesus. He often went to be alone to pray.
- Prayer includes adoration, thanksgiving, confession, intercession and petition.
- Prayer is an essential part of a Christian's relationship with God.

# The power of faith

## The epileptic boy

In the previous unit you read about the healing of the epileptic boy. There are many other things to note in the account of that miracle.

> When they came to the other disciples, they saw a large crowd around them and the teachers of the law arguing with them. As soon as all the people saw Jesus, they were overwhelmed with wonder and ran to greet him. 'What are you arguing with them about?' he asked them.
>
> A man in the crowd answered, 'Teacher, I brought you my son, who is possessed by an evil spirit that has robbed him of speech. Whenever it seizes him, it throws him to the ground. He foams at the mouth, gnashes his teeth and becomes rigid. I asked your disciples to drive out the spirit, but they could not.'
>
> 'O unbelieving generation,' Jesus replied, 'how long shall I stay with you? How long shall I put up with you? Bring the boy to me.' So they brought him. When the spirit saw Jesus, it immediately threw the boy into a convulsion. He fell to the ground and rolled around, foaming at the mouth. Jesus asked the boy's father, 'How long has he been like this?'
>
> 'From childhood,' he answered. 'It has often thrown him into fire or water to kill him. But if you can do anything, take pity on us and help us.'
>
> '"If you can"?' said Jesus. 'Everything is possible for him who believes.'
>
> Immediately the boy's father exclaimed, 'I do believe; help me overcome my unbelief!'
>
> When Jesus saw that a crowd was running to the scene, he rebuked the evil spirit. 'You deaf and mute spirit,' he said. 'I command you, come out of him and never enter him again.' The spirit shrieked, convulsed him violently and came out. The boy looked so much like a corpse that many said, 'He's dead'. But Jesus took him by the hand and lifted him to his feet, and he stood up. After Jesus had gone indoors, his disciples asked him privately, 'Why couldn't we drive it out?' He replied, 'This kind can come out only by prayer.' (9: 14-29)

- People of Jesus' day thought that much sickness and disability were caused by sin or evil spirits. This boy is said to have an evil spirit. A modern doctor would see things differently.

- The boy's problem is well described in the Gospel: he falls to the ground, he foams at the mouth, he grits his teeth, he becomes stiff all over, the attacks cause him to harm himself.

These symptoms would seem to suggest that the boy had epilepsy. Even if the miracle is about the healing of epilepsy, rather than exorcising an evil spirit, the early Church looked upon this incident as showing Jesus' ability and willingness to help those in need.

## The need for faith

Faith is at the centre of this miracle story and it concerns three groups of people.

1 The people who witnessed the incident needed faith. Jesus became angry with the people and their whole generation for not having faith.

2 The boy's father needed more faith. He had some faith, but felt that he had not enough to help his son. He needed help to strengthen his faith.

3 The disciples needed faith. They were surprised that they were not able to help the boy. Jesus says, 'Only prayer can drive this kind out, nothing else can'. A strong relationship with God was what they needed.

It was the father's faith which caused Jesus to respond. When he asked for his faith to be strengthened, Jesus saw that his faith was real. The little faith the man had was enough to cure the boy.

> The father of the epileptic boy said, 'I do believe; help me overcome my unbelief!' He meant 'I do have faith. Help me where my faith is not strong enough'.

## How can we describe faith?

Faith means having complete trust in God. It means believing in:

- the power of God – he is in control
- the love of God – he wants the best for us.

Faith is a personal response on behalf of the believer: Christians trust God with their life. This is an act of deep love, and love is at the heart of faith. If prayer is to be effective, then there must be faith.

In the Gospel, faith means placing complete trust in Jesus. Through Jesus, individuals called upon the power of God believing that He would help. In response to that faith, miracles take place.

Some people believe that miracles bring about faith. In Mark's Gospel this is not the case. Faith comes first, then the miracle. It is a deep and abiding faith in Christ as the Son of God that results in a response – a miracle.

- Faith is not unshakeable. There are times when it is not as strong as it is at others. The man's request that his faith be strengthened results in Jesus healing the boy. The little faith the man had was enough to cure the boy.
- Jesus' words, 'Everything is possible for the person who has faith', would have been as inspiring for the early Church as it is for Christians today.

At the time the Gospel was being written, the first followers of Jesus were being persecuted for their faith. Persecution against Christians continues today in many parts of the world. These words of Jesus, and others like them, have inspired great acts of courage and determination throughout the history of Christianity.

### Activities

1  Thought tracking: The epileptic boy, his father, a disciple and a member of the crowd. **C 2.1a, PS 2.2, 2.3, WO 2.2**

2  What is faith? What makes one person have faith in another? **PS 2.1**

### Key points

- To a Christian, faith is a total trust in God.
- Faith was essential before Jesus performed the miracle.
- Faith comes from a close relationship with God, a relationship that must be rooted in prayer.

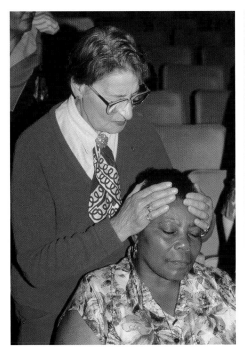

*Services of healing are carried out by a number of Christian traditions today.*

# Two miracles of healing

In 5: 21-43 two miracles are described together. Jesus heals one person while he is on the way to help another. These people are Jairus' daughter (5: 21-4, 35-43) and the woman who touched Jesus' cloak (5: 25-34).

## The power of faith and prayer

These stories have points in common.

- Both show faith and the belief that Jesus has the power to change a person's life.
- Both concern Jesus healing a woman. At that time, women were thought to be less important than men and socially inferior. These two miracles show that Jesus' love for humanity does not depend on gender. Everyone is equally important and can share in the power of God.
- Both involve people who could not be helped by the doctors of the day.

Although the two episodes are closely connected, they should be studied separately. As you study them, think about the following things:

- who is being healed, and of what?
- how does Jesus heal the person?
- what does Jesus say?
- what is the reaction of the witness?
- what does the miracle teach people today about the power of faith and prayer?

### Jairus' daughter

A large crowd gathered round Jesus while he was by the lake. Then one of the synagogue rulers, named Jairus, came there. Seeing Jesus, he fell at his feet and pleaded earnestly with him, 'My little daughter is dying. Please come and put your hands on her, so that she will be healed and live.' So Jesus went with him. (5: 21-4)

While Jesus was still speaking, some men came from the house of Jairus, the synagogue ruler. 'Your daughter is dead,' they said. 'Why bother the teacher any more?'

Ignoring what they said, Jesus told the synagogue ruler, 'Don't be afraid; just believe.' He did not let anyone follow him except Peter, James and John the brother of James. When they came to the home of the synagogue ruler, Jesus saw a commotion, with people crying and wailing loudly. He went in and said to them, 'Why all this commotion and wailing? The child is not dead but asleep.' But they laughed at him.

After he put them all out, he took the child's father and mother and the disciples who were with him, and went in where the child was. He took her by the hand and said to her, 'Talitha koum!' (which means, 'Little girl, I say to you, get up!'). Immediately the girl stood up and walked around (she was twelve years old). At this they were completely astonished. He gave strict orders not to let anyone know about this, and told them to give her something to eat.

- Jairus believed that Jesus had the power to save his daughter. Jesus noticed Jairus' faith and responded to it. It is because the father had faith that the girl made a complete recovery.
- As on two other highly important occasions (see 9: 2-13 and 14: 32-42) Jesus chose three of the twelve disciples to witness the miracle – Peter, James and John.
- Notice that in the story Jesus says Jairus' daughter is 'only sleeping'. Some people think that this refers to Jesus' belief that death is only a gentle passage into eternal life. Others say that Jesus knew that the girl was not dead, but was in a deep coma. 2000 years ago it was difficult to tell whether a person in a coma was alive or dead. In any case, a coma in those days usually resulted

in death. The early Christians looked upon this miracle as a sign of Jesus' power over death.

- Mark wanted to record the words of power Jesus used but, as most of his readers would not have spoken this language, he gave a translation of the Aramaic *'Talitha, koum'*.

- Jesus ordered the witnesses to tell no one about the miracle. (See glossary **Messianic secret**.)

- For Christians the miracle is a sign that God has the power to defeat death and his Son shares in that power.

## The woman who touched Jesus' cloak

A large crowd followed and pressed around him. And a woman was there who had been subject to bleeding for twelve years. She had suffered a great deal under the care of many doctors and had spent all she had, yet instead of getting better she grew worse. When she heard about Jesus, she came up behind him in the crowd and touched his cloak, because she thought, 'If I just touch his clothes I will be healed.' Immediately her bleeding stopped and she felt in her body that she was freed from her suffering.

At once Jesus realized that power had gone out from him. He turned around in the crowd and asked, 'Who touched my clothes?'

'You see the people crowding against you,' his disciples answered, 'and yet you can ask "Who touched me?"' But Jesus kept looking around to see who had one it. Then the woman, knowing what had happened to her, came and fell at his feet and, trembling with fear, told him the whole truth. He aid to her, 'Daughter, your faith has healed you. Go in peace and be freed from your suffering.' (5: 24-34)

- The woman believed that only Jesus could help her. She had tried everything else. Her faith and trust in him were so great that she believed she only had to touch his clothes to be made well.

- The woman's constant bleeding for twelve years may have been connected with her menstrual cycle. According to the Law of Moses, this made her unclean. If she touched a rabbi it would have made him unclean as well. She was trembling with fear when she owned up as she

must have wondered what Jesus' reaction would be.

- Jesus knew that someone had not just brushed against him in the crush of the crowd. He had been touched on purpose, and he had felt power go out of him.

- The woman's meeting with Jesus left her physically well. It also affected her spiritually; she is told to 'Go in peace'. Everything in her life is now well.

- Notice that Jesus calls the woman 'Daughter'. Her faith has 'saved' her; she is now a member of God's kingdom, a part of the family of God.

*Many Jewish women today take a ritual bath at the synagogue every month to make themselves ritually clean after menstruation.*

### Activities

1 The woman with a haemorrhage was considered to be an outcast in her society. Which groups of people today might be considered outcast and shunned by society? **PS 2.1**

2 Read Mark 8: 11-13. Why do you think Jesus refused to perform miracles for the Pharisees? What message does this story give to people today who ask God for a miracle? **PS 2.1**

### Key points

- The power of Jesus to heal is open to all, regardless of status, gender or condition.

- Christians believe Jesus responds to anyone who puts their faith and trust in him.

# The meaning of the miracles

## What is a miracle?

A miracle is a wonderful, mighty act beyond normal human powers. It is an extraordinary event by God or a supernatural force. It is an occurrence which goes against the usual laws of nature. Christians believe a miracle shows the intervention of God in their lives. A miracle is an event that, even in the twenty-first century, cannot always be explained by medical or scientific knowledge.

The miracles in Mark's Gospel are either healing miracles or nature miracles.

## Healing miracles

The accounts of the healing miracles follow this pattern:

- the setting of the event
- the manner in which the person is cured – by touch, by word or from a distance
- the reaction of those who witnessed the miracle.

The healing miracles you need to know about are:

- The man with an evil spirit (1: 21-8; see page 60)
- The paralyzed man (2: 1-12; see page 16)
- The man with the shrivelled hand (3: 1-6; see page 91)
- Jairus' daughter (5: 21-4, 35-43; see pages 64–5)
- The woman with a haemorrhage (5: 25-34; see page 65)
- The Syro-Phoenician woman's daughter (7: 24-30; see page 19)
- The epileptic boy (9: 14-29; see pages 61–2)
- Blind Bartimaeus (10: 46-52; see pages 20–1).

It was a common belief in those days that serious illness or disability was a punishment from God for sins committed either by the victims or their parents.

By healing so many people, Jesus showed that this was not the case – if it was, why would the Son undo the work of the Father? It is widely agreed in medical circles today that some illnesses can be caused by deep, spiritual anguish or guilt. Perhaps Jesus had this in mind when he said to the paralyzed man, 'My son, your sins are forgiven' (2: 5).

## Nature miracles

Jesus reveals his power over nature, and suspends the laws of the natural universe. Christians believe that Jesus is the Son of God and, as such, he has the power to command the forces he created. Many people find these miracles particularly difficult to accept.

The nature miracles you need to know about:

- Calming the storm (4: 35-41; see page 18)
- Feeding the 5000 (6: 30-44; see pages 18–19).

## Why did Mark include the miracles in his Gospel?

The miracles in the Gospels should not be understood as merely an historic record of an actual event. To the early Christians the miracles meant much more. They are proof of who Jesus was, of his overwhelming goodness, and of his connection with the Father who sent him. Mark used accounts of Jesus' miracles to show that:

- Jesus was the long-awaited Messiah
- he was the Son of God
- the kingdom of God was present on earth (for kingdom of God, see page 50)
- by putting their faith in Jesus, individuals' lives could be transformed.

## Why did Jesus perform miracles?

One could say that the easy answer to this is that Jesus was such a compassionate person that he could not stand by and watch the suffering of others.

As the Son of God Jesus had power and he used it to improve the quality of people's lives. But there is more to Jesus' actions than this. Love is at the heart of the Christian message, and one of the main points of Jesus' teachings was the deep and abiding love of God. He wants the best for his creation, and wishes his people to be well – physically, mentally and spiritually.

> When Jesus landed and saw a large crowd, he had compassion on them, because they were like sheep without a shepherd. (From the feeding of the 5000, 6: 34; see also 1: 41, 5: 19, 8: 2 and 9: 22.)

Jesus performed miracles in response to faith.

> 'Your faith has made you well. Go in peace, and be healed of your trouble' (to the woman with a haemorrhage, 5: 34).

## Difficulties of belief

Some modern readers have difficulty in accepting the gospel miracles as actual events. They may say that there is little evidence of miraculous happenings today and, therefore, pass off the stories in the gospels as belonging to a time of ignorance and misunderstanding, when anything out of the ordinary would be explained as an act of God or of an evil force. They may say, 'Prove that this happened and we will believe'.

Sometimes people believe that there is a natural explanation for miracles. For instance, in the healing of Jairus' daughter they take literally the words of Jesus 'The child is not dead – she is only sleeping'.

Others point to what they see as miracles that have taken place in recent years. After prayer, people for whom doctors have given up hope have made remarkable recoveries.

The 'proof' that Jesus performed miracles can only really be found in the New Testament. A Christian may argue that believing in the truth of the gospels is an act of faith. Would the gospel writers really set out to lead us down the wrong path? They wrote what they believed to be the truth from eye-witness accounts and from the teachings of the early Church.

*Padre Pio of Pietrelcina, who died in 1968. Some Christians claim that miracles of healing have taken place following requests for Padre Pio's prayers.*

### Activities

1  Hot seat: teacher as Mark in the hot seat. Students question on why he included particular miracles in the Gospel – or why he included any miracles at all. **C 2.1a**

2  Why do some people have difficulty believing in the miracles of Jesus? How might a Christian answer them? **PS 2.1**

### Key points

- The early Christians believed that the miracles are proof that Jesus was both the Messiah and the Son of God.
- The miracles were Jesus' response to faith and to human need.

## Healing ministries today

People may have heard of the healing miracles Jesus performed 2000 years ago, but they may not realise or believe that such things can happen today. Christians claim that Jesus can bring wholeness of body, mind and spirit today through faith and prayer. The Church continues the healing ministry of Jesus throughout the world. This healing ministry is carried out in a number of ways.

### *Praying for God's healing power to help a person*

People may continue the healing ministry of Jesus by praying for those who are suffering. A number of Christian traditions hold services of healing.

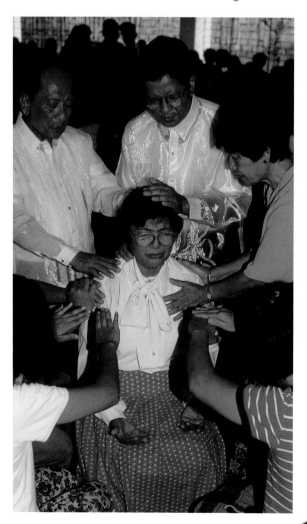

Individuals receive the 'laying on of hands' and are prayed for by the congregation. The priest or minister lays their hands on the person, symbolizing the healing touch of Jesus. At this point in the service, words such as these may be used:

In the name of God and trusting in his might alone,
receive Christ's healing touch to make you whole.
May Christ bring you wholeness
of body, mind and spirit,
deliver you from every evil,
and give you peace.
Amen.

(Taken from *Healing Rites for Common Worship*,
Church of England)

### *Pilgrimages to places of healing*

Many Christians visit places in different parts of the world where prayers are said for those who are very sick. These may be places where miracles of healing have occurred. Such a place is Lourdes, a French town at the foot of the Pyrenees.

For a period of six months in 1858, a young girl called Bernadette Soubirous had a number of visions of the Virgin Mary in a grotto near to her home in Lourdes. In 1862, these visions were declared authentic by the Pope, and it was said that the underground spring revealed to Bernadette had miraculous healing qualities. Since then, Lourdes has become a major pilgrimage centre. Almost 3 million people visit the grotto every year to pray for others or to be prayed for themselves.

### *A vocation to heal*

Many Christians have a **vocation** to help those who are ill in a practical way. A vocation is an occupation to which someone feels called to dedicate themselves. Christian medical workers may feel called to dedicate their lives to heal and ease the suffering of others, in their own country or in other countries around the world. In this way, these Christians may feel that they are spreading the good news of Jesus and of his concern for those in need.

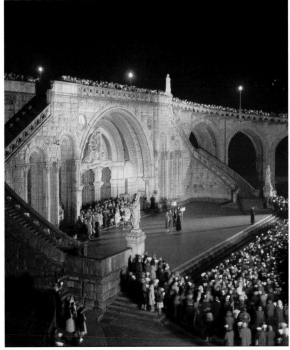

*An evening candlelit procession at Lourdes is an unforgettable experience.*

1 Visit http://olrl.org/stories/lourdes.html and www.ewtn.com/library/MARY/ ZLOURDES.HTM. Choose one healing described on one of these websites. Summarize the account you have chosen. Is it an example of a modern miracle? Give reasons for your answer. **IT 2.1, 2.2, PS 2.2, 2.3**

2 Would you expect a Christian surgeon to pray before performing a major operation? Give reasons for your answer. **PS 2.1**

## Key points

- The Christian belief that faith and prayer can bring about healing is as strong today as it was 2000 years ago.

# Exam questions to practise

Below are some sample exam questions on faith and prayer. The first two have examiner's tips to give you some hints on how to score full marks. The others are for you to try on your own. A good idea is to work out your own hints on how to score full marks before answering them.

1  **(a)** Describe the healing of the epileptic boy (the boy with an evil spirit)? (6)
   **(b)** How does the incident show the importance Jesus attached to faith and prayer? (4)

2  Do you think it is important for Christians to believe that Jesus really did perform miracles? Give reasons for your answer, showing you have considered more than one point of view. (5)

Now try these questions with no hints. Before you write an answer try to write down your own hints on how to score full marks.

3  Give two examples of occasions when Jesus prayed. What special reason to pray had he on each occasion? (8)

4  Why is the woman with a haemorrhage considered an excellent example of a person with faith? (4)

## How to score full marks

1  This is a question to test what you know and understand. In (a) the description will be marked on levels of response. In (b) you will need to make specific points concerning both faith *and* prayer.

2  This is a question to test evaluation. It will be marked on levels of response. Be sure to consider at least two approaches.

# Discipleship and leadership

**This section includes:**

- The twelve disciples
- The nature and cost of discipleship
- The mission of the Twelve
- Peter's promise and denial
- The mission to the modern World
- The life of a modern Christian
- The life of a modern Christian community

Jesus chose twelve disciples to be with him, so that he could prepare them to carry on his mission when he had left them. He taught them about the demands of discipleship. He sent them on a mission so that they might experience for themselves what discipleship meant, in practical terms. They were ordinary human beings with failings, as Peter showed when he denied Jesus, but he still trusted in them.

Christians today see themselves as having a mission to the modern world. The section contains examples of modern Christians and the ways in which they serve Jesus.

## Disciples and apostles

A **disciple** is someone who believes in and helps to spread the teachings of another. It is someone who learns from a religious leader, and who wishes to live life according to the leader's wishes and commands. At times, these men are called 'apostles'. An **apostle** is someone who is 'sent' to carry out the wishes of another. In Mark's Gospel, the disciples are called apostles whenever they are sent out by Jesus on a mission of teaching and healing.

The first thing Jesus did at the start of his mission was to choose men from among his followers to be disciples. He wanted them to be close to him and to learn from him. They were called for three main reasons:

- to be trained for the task of sharing in Jesus' mission
- to be the first group of followers who would bring others into the community
- to be the ones to continue Jesus' mission after he had gone.

The disciples were often taught privately by Jesus; he explained his teachings in great depth when they were alone. He also found the time to teach them away from the crowds on what it means to be a disciple (8: 31-10: 52).

## The call of the first four

In the first chapter of the Gospel, Jesus calls upon four fishermen to drop what they are doing and follow him.

As Jesus walked beside the Sea of Galilee, he saw Simon and his brother Andrew casting a net into the lake, for they were fishermen.

'Come, follow me', Jesus said, 'and I will make you fishers of men.' At once they left their nets and followed him.

When he had gone a little farther, he saw James son of Zebedee and his brother John in a boat, preparing their nets. Without delay he called them, and they left their father Zebedee in the boat with the hired men and followed him. (1: 16-20)

The story of the call of Jesus' first disciples contains a number of important points.

- Jesus called them individually. His great power and **charisma** drew them to him.
- Their response was immediate. They stopped what they were doing and, without discussion, followed him.
- Jesus told them that he would help them to be 'fishers of men'. They would bring people into the family of God.
- The story is an important reminder for Mark's readers that discipleship may mean leaving everything behind to follow the Christian way of life. God's call is more important than anything else.

*Four of Jesus' disciples were fishermen. He called them to be 'fishers of men'.*

- Peter, James and John have sometimes been called 'The Inner Three' disciples. It would seem that, of the twelve disciples, they were particularly close to Jesus, and were chosen to witness three extraordinary events in Jesus' ministry:
  - the raising of Jairus' daughter (5: 21-4, 35-43)
  - Jesus' Transfiguration (9: 2-13)
  - Jesus at prayer in the Garden of Gethsemane (14: 32-42).

## Choosing the disciples

Jesus went up on a mountainside and called to him those he wanted, and they came to him. He appointed twelve – designating them apostles – that they might be with him and that he might send them out to preach and to have authority to drive out demons.

These are the twelve he appointed: Simon (to whom he gave the name Peter); James son of Zebedee and his brother John (to them he gave the name Boanerges, which means Sons of Thunder); Andrew, Philip, Bartholomew, Matthew, Thomas, James son of Alphaeus, Thaddaeus, Simon the Zealot and Judas Iscariot, who betrayed him. (3: 13-19)

After he had healed a man with a shrivelled hand, the pharisees and members of King Herod's party (the Herodians) began to plan how they might have Jesus executed (3: 1-6). This led Jesus to go away for a while to the hills with a small band of followers. It was from among this band that Jesus chose his other disciples.

- He chose them to be his close companions.
- He sent them out to preach in his name.
- He gave them the ability to drive out evil spirits.

The fact that Jesus chose *twelve* disciples may be symbolic. In the Old Testament Jacob, one of the great patriarchs of the Jewish faith, had twelve sons. They became the founders of the twelve tribes of Israel. By choosing twelve disciples, Jesus may have been suggesting that he had been sent by God for all the Jewish people.

Jesus did not choose wealthy or influential men to be his disciples. In fact, at first glance, his choice seems rather strange:

- one (Matthew) was a social outcast, a tax collector; hated by the Jewish people because of his work for the Romans
- four (Peter, Andrew, James, John) were fishermen, used to living a hard way of life, and with little influence in Jewish society
- two (James and John) seemed to suffer from tempers. Jesus named them 'Sons of Thunder'
- one (Simon) was a member of the Zealot party, a violent group which fought against the Roman occupation of Israel.

Jesus could see into the hearts of these men; he was able to look below the surface and see their true qualities. Christians may take comfort from this. They believe God calls all types of people to his service; what may seem like failings to us can be used by God, and turned into strengths.

### Activities

1 In pairs discuss the following question: you and four other members of your school have been asked to clear and repair a rundown children's playground in the town. Which four people would you choose to have with you? Give reasons why. **C 2.1a, WO 2.1, 2.2**

2 Why do you think Jesus chose the type of men he did to be his disciples? If Jesus were choosing disciples today, what types of people might he select? **PS 2.1**

### Key points

- Jesus called twelve men from among his followers to be his disciples.
- He chose them to be his companions and to continue his work after he had gone.
- None of them had a particularly high place in Jewish society. They were 'ordinary' men.

# The nature and cost of discipleship

## The nature of discipleship

Discipleship is an important theme in Mark's Gospel. It is as important for Christians today as it was for the first disciples of Jesus.

True discipleship is not something that can be done in a half-hearted way. To Christians, it means giving all that they have in the service of God and of other people. This is clearly explained in the story of the widow at the treasury in 12: 41-4.

> Jesus sat down opposite the place where the offerings were put and watched the crowd putting their money into the temple treasury. Many rich people threw in large amounts. But a poor widow came and put in two very small copper coins, worth only a fraction of a penny.
>
> Calling his disciples to him, Jesus said, 'I tell you the truth, this poor widow has put more into the treasury than all the others. They all gave out of their wealth; but she, out of her poverty, put in everything all she had to live on.

*Discipleship: giving time and money to help others.*

There are a number of important points in this story:

- Jesus neither criticized nor praised the rich people who put large amounts of money into the offering box, even though it was money they probably had to spare.

- The widow is praised because she gave more than anyone else to God. Her offering was very small, but it was all that she had.

- We all have different levels of ability and talent.

In this story Jesus teaches that a person who commits everything they have to the service of God, however little that might be, is more precious to God than someone who has great ability and resources, but is less committed. Real Christian discipleship requires total commitment.

## The cost of discipleship

About halfway through his ministry, Jesus began to warn his disciples that his work for God would result in his suffering and death. He knew that his teachings and popularity would be seen as a threat by his enemies. He also realized that life would be made difficult for those who believed that he was the Messiah sent by God. They, too, had to be prepared to suffer for their beliefs and discipleship.

> Jesus called the crowd to him along with his disciples and said, 'If anyone would come after me, he must deny himself and take up his cross and follow me. For whoever wants to save his life will lose it, but whoever loses his life for me and for the gospel will save it. What good is it for a man to gain the whole world, yet forfeit his soul? Or what can a man give in exchange for his soul? If anyone is ashamed of me and my words in this adulterous and sinful generation, the Son of Man will be ashamed of him when he comes in his Father's glory with the holy angels. (8: 34-8)

There are a number of important ideas in this passage which need to be studied in turn. First, Jesus said that those who wish to follow him must deny self, take up the cross and follow him.

What did Jesus mean? What would his words have meant to his first disciples, and what do they mean for Christians today?

1  *To deny self* means that Jesus' followers should always put other people's needs before their own. Disciples should not be concerned about social position, or have so much ambition that they need to be first in everything. Christian disciples should put their own needs and wishes last.

**2** *To take up the cross* is probably one of the most challenging commands of Jesus. Mark was writing his gospel at a time when many Christians were dying for their belief in Jesus. Crucifixion was a real possibility. There have been times since then, even to the present day, when Christians have been **persecuted** for their beliefs. Everyone tries to avoid suffering, but there may come a time in a Christian's life when suffering and persecution are an inevitable result of faith in Jesus Christ. True Christian discipleship means being prepared to accept this suffering, even if it leads to death.

**3** *To follow him* means accepting the Christian way of life and treading in the footsteps of Jesus, following his example as closely as possible. Obedience to the will of God and putting others first may lead to suffering, as it did for Jesus. However, the invitation to 'follow me' also holds the promise of sharing in Christ's resurrected life.

Next, Jesus says:

*'Whoever wants to save his life will lose it, but whoever loses his life for me and the gospel will save it.'*

Jesus is speaking of those who do not follow him because they fear mockery or suffering. Others fear to declare their faith in public. Rather than saving their life, they actually risk losing eternal life. Those who remain faithful will share in the resurrection of Christ.

*'What good is it for a man to gain the whole world, yet forfeit his soul?'*

A person may dedicate their life to achieving wealth, power and comfort and, in doing so, neglect to follow the teachings of Jesus. What is the point of this? Such a person will lose everything in the end, and will not receive eternal life.

*'If anyone is ashamed of me and my words … the Son of Man will be ashamed of him …'*

If a Christian is not prepared to publicly declare faith in Jesus, then Jesus will be ashamed of that person on the Day of Judgement.

Modern Christians believe that they are disciples of Jesus. They consider it important to learn the teachings of Jesus and to put them into practice in their daily lives. He is their example of a life lived according to the wishes of God; a role model. Christians believe that eternal life is possible for those who choose to follow the teachings and example of Jesus Christ.

✝ **Tuesday 7 November**

# TURKMENISTAN

Currently, there are only about 400 indigenous Christians in Turkmenistan, and the average age of the believers is 24. Over the last few years, all expatriate Christians in the country have been expelled, leaving this fledgling Church isolated and cut off.

*Open Doors Prayer Diary, November 2000.*

## Activities

**1** Choose a cause for which Christians might think it worth suffering and even dying. Explain the reasons for your choice. **PS 2.1**

**2** Visit the website of an organization which tries to help and support Christians who are being persecuted. (Open Doors (www.od.org/oduk) or Aid to the Church in Need (www.kirche-in-not.org) are organizations helping persecuted Christians.) Make notes on at least two of these Christians organizations. **IT 2.1, 2.2, PS 2.2, 2.3**

## Key points

● Discipleship is an important subject in Mark's Gospel.

● A disciple is someone who wishes to follow the will of God.

● A disciple follows the example of Jesus. This sometimes leads to suffering and even death.

● Real discipleship is rewarded with eternal life.

● Disciples put the needs of others before their own.

## The disciples spread the gospel

During Jesus' ministry, the twelve disciples were sent out on a journey to spread the news of the kingdom of God. They were to go in different directions and in twos, for safety reasons. The disciples would have been called 'apostles' at this point, because they were being sent to do his work. Before they went, Jesus gave them clear instructions.

> Calling the twelve to him, he sent them out two by two and gave them authority over evil spirits. These were his instructions: 'Take nothing for the journey except a staff – no bread, no bag, no money in your belts. Wear sandals but not an extra tunic. Whenever you enter a house, stay there until you leave that town. And if any place will not welcome you or listen to you, shake the dust off your feet when you leave, as a testimony against them.'
> They went out and preached that people should repent. They drove out many demons and anointed many sick people with oil and healed them. (6: 7-13)

Jesus' instructions fall into two parts. First, he gave instructions as to what the disciples should pack for their journey.

| They *could* take | a walking stick |
| | a pair of sandals. |
| They *could not* take | food |
| | a bag |
| | money |
| | another coat. |

### Why did he give these instructions?

At first glance, Jesus' instructions seem rather harsh. After all, the items he told them not to pack would have been considered essential for a long journey. One reason could be that Jesus wanted the disciples to travel light; heavy luggage would have slowed them down and they would not have been able to travel long distances easily on foot.

Another suggestion is that by taking so little with them, the disciples would have had to learn to depend on God and the generosity of other people for everything. An important part of discipleship is the willingness to be dependent on God; to trust that he will provide through others. Jesus also gave instructions on where the disciples should stay whilst they were travelling.

- Whenever shelter was offered to them, they were to stay in that house until they were ready to move on to another area. Changing houses in the same area was thought to be impolite.

- If the people of a town did not welcome the disciples, they were not to waste time. They were told to move on, and to shake the town's dust off their feet as they left. This would be a sign to the people of the town that the disciples had no time for them because they had rejected God and the teachings of Christ.

The disciples were sent on their missionary journey to do three things:

- to tell people that they should repent of their sins and turn back to God
- to drive out evil spirits
- to anoint sick people with oil and heal them.

### What this story means for modern Christians

Many Christians today go out into the world to spread the news of the kingdom of God in much the same way as the twelve disciples. They are called **missionaries**. Although life has changed a great deal since the earliest days of Christianity, Jesus' teachings are as relevant today as they were 2000 years ago. If a person feels called by God to preach the Christian message abroad or in their own country, they need to learn to trust in God and not to be weighed down by material worries. The belief that God will provide for all their basic needs through the generosity of others has been a real experience for many Christians.

There are a number of Christian organizations which carry on the work of the disciples in the world today. These include Tear Fund, Christian Aid, TROCAIRE, CAFOD, and various missionary societies.

## The rewards of discipleship

It is important to understand that being a Christian does not mean accepting a life of misery and constant suffering. Quite the opposite is true, as can be seen in the words of Jesus in 10: 28-31. Peter asked Jesus how he and the other disciples would be rewarded for following him.

> Peter said to him, 'We have left everything to follow you!'
> 'I tell you the truth,' Jesus replied, 'no one who has left home or brothers or sisters or mother or father or children or fields for me and the gospel will fail to receive a hundred times as much in this present age (homes, brothers, sisters, mothers, children, fields – and with them, persecutions) and in the age to come, eternal life'.

Jesus teaches that those who whole-heartedly decide to follow a Christian way of life will be rewarded many times over. Christians feel that, by following the example of Jesus, their lives are enriched. A close relationship with God, and the fellowship that can be found within the Church community, are among the rewards of discipleship. But the greatest reward of all for Christians is Jesus' promise of eternal life.

*'To do the work we do for thirty years or more requires an enormously high level of commitment. We describe our lifestyle in Covenant Players as "living on the cutting edge of faith". This "living" can be as basic as trusting God for a bed and food for that day, to the strengthening of one's resolve in learning a role.'*

*Trócaire carries on the mission of the twelve disciples by preaching the Christian message, feeding the hungry, looking after the sick, and fighting against injustice in the world.*

### Activities

1 Hot seat: the teacher represents a Christian missionary. Students question the missionary about what impels them to leave the relative comfort of home and take the Christian message to other parts of the world. (If it is possible to invite a missionary to visit the class, even better.) **C 2.1a, WO 2.2, 2.3**

2 The Covenant Players are actors who go out in small groups to perform Christian drama in schools, churches, homes, prisons – anywhere where people will listen to their message. They rely to a great extent on the hospitality they are offered – beds for the night and meals. Visit their website (www.covenantplayers.org) and make notes on what they do – and, more importantly, why. **IT 2.1, 2.2, PS 2.1**

### Key points

- Jesus sent his disciples on a mission to spread the gospel.
- By insisting they took very little with them he made them trust in God and the generosity of others.
- The greatest reward of discipleship for all Christians is Jesus' promise of eternal life.

## The importance of Peter

Simon, later known as Peter, has an important position among the disciples in Mark's Gospel. He is the first and the last disciple to be mentioned, and his name occurs 25 times.

Peter seems to have been the spokesman for the disciples. For example, it was Peter who:

- answered for the group when Jesus asked them who they thought he was (8: 27-30)

- questioned the need for Jesus' suffering and death (8: 31-3)

- offered to build tents for Jesus, Moses and Elijah on the mountain of the Transfiguration (9: 2-8)

- followed Jesus after his arrest when the other disciples ran away (14: 53-4)

- suffered greatly after denying that he knew Jesus (14: 66-72).

Following the resurrection of Jesus, Peter became the leader of the apostles – the 'rock' on which the Christian Church was built. Peter's memories of the time he spent with Jesus were used by Mark when he wrote his Gospel.

*Peter is mentioned more times in Mark's Gospel than any other disciple. He became the leader of the apostles after the resurrection of Jesus.*

## The disciples had their faults

Mark does not hide Peter's weaknesses. Peter was an ordinary man. Like everyone, he made mistakes. In fact this Gospel, more than any other, shines a spotlight on the times when the disciples failed in understanding, faith and courage. Here are a few examples:

- in the calming of the storm (4: 35-41), Jesus commented on the disciples' lack of faith in his ability to keep them safe – 'Why are you so afraid? Do you still have no faith?'

- in the story of the request of James and John (10: 35-45), Jesus had to explain again the true meaning of discipleship. It is not to achieve personal glory, but to put others first in all things

- when Jesus predicted that he would be betrayed and put to death, the disciples did not understand what he meant and were afraid to ask him about it (9: 30-2)

- in the Garden of Gethsemane (14: 32-52), Peter, James and John fell asleep three times. Jesus had asked them to keep watch for him while he prayed. When Jesus was arrested, all the disciples ran away in fear

- at Jesus' crucifixion (15: 21-41), none of the disciples were there to support him.

## Peter's promise to Jesus

Perhaps the most dramatic example of the disciples failing in their duty to Jesus was the denial of Peter on the night before Jesus died. After Jesus had finished eating his Last Supper with the disciples, he took them to the Mount of Olives. He told them that they would all turn away from him, and that he would wait for them in Galilee after he had risen from the dead.

> When they had sung a hymn, they went out to the Mount of Olives. 'You will all fall away,' Jesus told them, 'for it is written: "I will strike the shepherd, and the sheep will be scattered." But after I have risen, I will go ahead of you into Galilee.'

Peter declared, 'Even if all fall away, I will not'. 'I tell you the truth', Jesus answered, 'today – yes, tonight – before the cock crows twice you yourself will disown me three times'. But Peter insisted emphatically, 'Even if I have to die with you, I will never disown you'. And all the others said the same. (14: 26-31)

These were brave words from Peter, and he probably meant what he said at the time. Little did he know that, a few hours later, his life would be in danger, and that he would deny that he even knew who Jesus was to save himself.

## Peter's denial

Peter had secretly followed Jesus and the crowd to the courtyard of the temple where Jesus was to be questioned by the Sanhedrin. He waited outside to see what was going to happen to Jesus.

While Peter was below in the courtyard, one of the servant girls of the high priest came by. When she saw Peter warming himself, she looked closely at him. 'You also were with that Nazarene, Jesus', she said. But he denied it. 'I don't know or understand what you're talking about', he said, and went out into the entrance.

When the servant girl saw him there, she said again to those standing around, 'This fellow is one of them'. Again he denied it.

After a little while, those standing near said to Peter, 'Surely you are one of them, for you are a Galilean'.

He began to call down curses on himself, and he swore to them, 'I don't know this man you're talking about'.

*Jesus predicted that Peter would deny knowing him to save his own life.*

Immediately the cock crowed the second time. Then Peter remembered the words Jesus had spoken to him: 'Before the cock crows twice you will disown me three times'. And he broke down and wept'. (14: 66-72)

Jesus had been right! Peter's courage had failed him. He should not be judged too harshly for this, the danger to his life was very real. At that time, the friends and followers of those who were found guilty of treason were often imprisoned or even executed. Peter would have known this. However, his feelings of guilt and despair immediately after the incident are obvious. He had failed the greatest test of discipleship, and he had failed a close friend.

## What this story means for modern Christians

Christians feel that they can take comfort in Mark's presentation of discipleship. Being a disciple of Jesus is not easy in any generation; all Christians experience times of anxiety and even despair when they feel that they have let God down in some way. Peter's story is seen as an example of how to deal with such a situation. He did not give in to his despair. He picked himself up and became a leading figure in the Church after the resurrection of Jesus. What is also important is that God forgave Peter for his denial. When the angel of the Lord told the women at the empty tomb that Jesus had risen from the dead, he particularly told them to tell Peter the good news (16: 7).

### Activities

1 Forum theatre: Peter, serving girl and bystander. **C 2.1a, WO 2.1, 2.2**

2 What evidence have you found that Peter helped Mark to write his Gospel? **PS 2.1, 2.3**

### Key points

- Jesus' disciples sometimes failed in their discipleship.
- Christians believe that God forgives mistakes.

# The mission to the modern world

## Preaching

Jesus' command that the good news be preached throughout the world has been taken up by many Christians. Some feel that they have a vocation, that they have been called to spread the Christian faith as priests, ministers, nuns and monks. Others believe that they can serve Christ in their daily lives as laity, passing on the good news to those they meet.

## Missionary work

Christian missionaries travel to teach about Jesus. They also give practical help to the communities in which they stay. This might include building schools and medical centres, helping those suffering from the effects of natural disasters and teaching new skills to developing communities.

### Jesus' commission to the modern Church

Jesus' disciples in every generation are told to:
– 'go into the world and preach the good news'
– 'baptize believers'
– 'drive out demons'
– 'place your hands on sick people.'

## Healing ministry

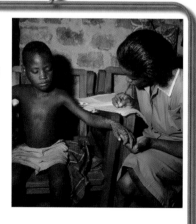

Many Christians feel compelled to spread the message of God's love through caring for those who are sick and in need of medical help in all areas of the world.

## Fighting injustice and prejudice

Christians believe that it is their duty to put other people before themselves. They feel that it is right to help those who are suffering at the hands of others throughout the world. Christians can be found in such organizations as Amnesty International and Greenpeace.

# The Church's commission

In the final chapter of Mark's Gospel, Jesus gives his last instructions, his commission, to the disciples. These instructions are also important for those who wish to become Christian disciples in any generation.

> Go into all the world and preach the good news to all creation. Whoever believes and is baptized will be saved, but whoever does not believe will be condemned. And these signs will accompany those who believe: In my name they will drive out demons; they will speak in new tongues; they will pick up snakes with their hands; and when they drink deadly poison, it will not hurt them at all; they will place their hands on sick people, and they will get well. (16: 15-18)

The apostles took Jesus' commission to heart. The New Testament book, Acts of the Apostles, tells the story of how the 'good news' about Jesus was carried to many places in the Middle East and into Europe. Communities of Christians sprang up in many areas, and these groups came to be known as Churches. The Christian Church was born!

## Activities

1 Hot seat: the teacher represents a priest, minister, nun or monk. Students question him/her on the life-choice they have made. (If one of these people could visit the class, even better.) **C 2.1a**

2 Visit www.greenpeace.org.uk and note what the organization does and why. Do you think the organization's aims and activities are compatible with Christian beliefs? Give reasons for your answer. **IT 2.1, 2.2**

## Key points

- Christians today obey the commission which Jesus gave to the apostles.
- Some feel they have a vocation to serve God in a particular way through:
  a preaching
  b missionary work
  c fighting injustice and prejudice
  d healing ministry.

## Putting the commandments into practice

Jesus' commission to those who wish to follow him, to be his disciples, is based on two principles. Christians should:

- 'Love the Lord your God with all your heart, with all your soul, with all your mind, and with all your strength'
- 'Love your neighbour as you love yourself'. (12: 28-34. See pages 56–7– kingdom of God)

There have been many individuals throughout the history of Christianity who have based their lives on these commandments. Some have done as much as they can in a quiet way, while the extraordinary actions of others have made them household names throughout the world.

## Mother Teresa of Calcutta

Mother Teresa was born Agnes Gonxha Bojaxhiu in 1910. She grew up the youngest of three children in Skopje, Macedonia.

When she was 18 years old, she decided to become a nun and joined the Sisters of Our Lady of Loreto in Ireland. When she entered the convent in Dublin she chose the name of Sister Teresa. By becoming a nun, she had made the decision to give up all her possessions, her family and friends, and dedicate her life to the service of God. In the same year, Teresa was sent to another convent owned by her order in Darjeeling, India. It was here that she continued her training as a nun.

A year later, in 1929, she was sent to Calcutta in India to teach at a school for girls. Although she was happy with her life and duties, Teresa was shocked by the poverty and disease which surrounded her school. Then, on a long train journey to Darjeeling in 1946, she felt that she was being called by God to change the direction of her life:

> I realised that I had the call to take care of the sick and the dying, the hungry, the naked, the homeless – to be God's Love in action to the poorest of the poor.

### The Missionaries of Charity

This was a milestone in Sister Teresa's life. She asked permission to leave the Loreto order and to establish a new order of nuns, the Missionaries of Charity. She received permission from Pope Pius XII and went into the streets of Calcutta with a few of her friends. Her only possession was a white sari with blue stripes.

In 1952 Mother Teresa and her fellow Missionaries of Charity began the work for which they have been famous ever since. Mother Teresa described how she managed to acquire her first centre for the desperately ill in Calcutta:

> I found a woman lying in the gutter in the middle of Calcutta. She was half eaten up by rats and ants. I took her to the hospital, but they could do nothing for her. They only took her because I refused to go home unless something was done for her. After they cared for her, I went straight to the town hall and asked for a place where I could take these people, because that day I found more people dying in the street. The employee of health services brought me to a Hindu temple. The building was empty and he asked me if I wanted it. I was glad with the offer for many reasons, but especially because it was the centre of prayer for Hindus.

The temple was renamed Nirmal Hriday, meaning 'Pure Heart'. It became a home for the sick and dying of Calcutta. Mother Teresa and her fellow nuns gathered desperately ill people off the streets and brought them to Nirmal Hriday so that they could either be healed, or spend their last days surrounded by comfort and love. Since that time, more than 42 000 people from Calcutta have been taken to Nirmal Hriday.

### Work throughout the world

Mother Teresa and the Missionaries of Charity have founded many centres throughout the world to help lessen people's suffering. These include:

- orphanages for babies and young children, who have been found in the street or have been brought to the centres from hospitals

- care settlements for those suffering from leprosy. Lepers are shunned by society in India; they are not allowed to work and many are evicted from their homes by their families. Mother Teresa had villages built where lepers could live and be cared for in peace

- houses for alcoholics, drug addicts, those suffering from AIDS and the homeless

- soup kitchens for the homeless in many large cities around the world

- rehabilitation houses for men and women released from prison

- many houses around the world where the Missionaries of Charity care for the dying. Their patients may have no one else to look after them, or they may not be able to afford medical treatment.

Mother Teresa died in 1997, but her work continues around the world in the community of nuns she founded, the Missionaries of Charity.

Mother Teresa once said:

> It is not how much we do, but how much love we put in the doing. It is not how much we give, but how much love we put in the giving.

Her words echo the theme of an incident in Mark's Gospel which we have covered in this section on discipleship. Can you name the incident? What are the similarities?

Mother Teresa dedicated her life to the service of God and of people in need. She saw all people as children of God and treated them as such. For Mother Teresa, the Christian emphasis on love was all-important. It was the foundation of her life and work. She once explained the work of the Missionaries of Charity:

> We want to bring the joy and love of God to the people. We want to bring them God himself, who gives them his love through us. At the same time we love God and show him our love by serving him in his people. We are not another organization of the Social Service; we have to be more, to give more – we have to give ourselves.

## Activities

1 Refer back to Jesus' teachings on the nature, cost and rewards of discipleship (pages 74–5). Having read the summary of Mother Teresa's work, make a careful note of the ways in which her life reflects Jesus' teachings about discipleship. **PS 2.2, 2.3**

2 Visit the website www.ascension-research .org/teresa.html. How is Mother Teresa's work being continued today? **IT 2.1, 2.2**

## Key points

- Many individuals have followed Jesus' teaching about discipleship.

- By setting up various agencies in different places, Mother Teresa has made it possible for other people to be disciples.

# The life of a modern Christian community

## Christians working together

Mother Teresa is an example of a Christian whose work is known throughout the world. Her discipleship was unique in that she used her position as a world famous figure to help others. However, a vital part of that work was her founding of a community, the Missionaries of Charity. In that way she enabled others to exercise their discipleship.

There are many other communities or organizations around the world whose members are committed to serving God and their neighbour. Examples of ways in which they serve others are:

- feeding the hungry
- caring for the sick
- working for peace
- fighting injustice.

One such organisation is the Corrymeela Community in Ireland.

Corrymeela, a Christian community in Northern Ireland.

Religious and political differences have divided the people of Northern Ireland for many years.

### How did Corrymeela begin?

The inspiration to set up Corrymeela began with one man's experiences during World War II. Ray Davey was a Christian YMCA volunteer, working in Libya close to the North African front. He was captured by German soldiers and taken to prisoner of war camps in Italy and Germany.

In the camps, Ray discovered that his fellow prisoners were suffering badly from the effects of boredom, loneliness and their uncertain future. Some prisoners were so depressed that they took to their beds and refused to eat. Ray encouraged them to meet in small groups. They talked about their homes, their families and their experiences during the war. They shared their fears and hopes for the future. As they talked, their depression began to lift. Men from many different religious and social backgrounds started to help each other, and their differences were forgotten as they supported each other in their captivity. Ray had formed a community.

In the years following the war, Ray worked amongst divided communities using the ideas that had been so successful in the prisoner of war camp. With the help of volunteers, many of them young people, he proved that Jesus' teachings on peace and reconciliation can work in the modern world. A centre was built at Ballycastle in Northern Ireland and named the Corrymeela Community.

When the troubles between Protestants and Roman Catholics flared up in 1968 in Northern Ireland, the community decided to concentrate on working for peace. Under Ray's leadership,

Corrymeela became a centre which offered the chance for people from both sides of the divide to meet together, to learn about each other, and to build bridges of peace. The Corrymeela community work to bring about reconciliation and forgiveness. They follow the example of Jesus who made friends with 'enemies' and asked his followers to do the same.

## Corrymeela at work

Corrymeela is on the Antrim coast of Northern Ireland. It is in a beautiful setting on a hill above Ballycastle, overlooking the Atlantic Ocean. The Christian community who live there are dedicated to working for peace and reconciliation in Northern Ireland.

- The community is made up of Protestants and Roman Catholics. They live together, work together, worship together. In other words, it is a living example of the way in which people of different beliefs can live together in peace and understanding.

- It is a place where people can meet to discuss their differences. Over 7000 people visit Corrymeela every year to discuss the political and religious issues at the heart of the Northern Ireland conflict. They can discuss them in an atmosphere of mutual respect and trust.

- Volunteers at Corrymeela offer help to individuals caught up in the troubles in Northern Ireland.

- The centre works in partnership with schools, youth groups and churches, bringing the young people of divided communities together. The aim of the community is to help young people discover ways of breaking down the barriers of prejudice and misunderstanding that exist in their communities.

Travelling The Road of Faith
Worship Resources from the Corrymeela Community

*Christians of all traditions join in the daily worship at Corrymeela.*

Families come to Corrymeela to escape the problems and tensions of their ordinary lives. For some families Corrymeela provides a rare, much-needed holiday. Single mothers, Protestant and Catholic, come for a weekend together with their children. The mothers have a chance to talk among themselves and this increases understanding. However, the main purpose is to allow them a time of relaxation and peace.

What makes the greatest impression on some visitors is the warmth and understanding. One mother was worried that people at Corrymeela would be annoyed with her rather noisy children. In the event, whenever the children misbehaved people went up to talk to them or to find something interesting for them to do. A rather shy child became much more outgoing because everyone was so friendly.

### Activities

1 Visit the Corrymeela website, www.corrymeela.org.uk and make notes about the work of the Community. In particular, look out for comments from people who have been helped by the community in some way. **IT 2.1, 2.2**

2 Forum theatre: a Catholic single parent, a Protestant single parent, a member of Corrymeela Community in informal conversation. What might they talk about? **C 2.1a, WO 2.1, 2.2**

### Key points

- The Corrymeela Community is an example of Christian discipleship in action in the tense and violent situation in Northern Ireland.

- The community teaches – and puts into practice – Jesus' teaching about loving your neighbour.

# Exam questions to practise

Below are some sample exam questions on discipleship. The first two have examiner's tips to give you some hints on how to score full marks. The others are for you to try on your own. A good idea is to work out your own hints on how to score full marks before answering them.

**1** **(a)** What promise did Peter make to Jesus at the Last Supper? Describe how he failed to keep that promise. (8)

**(b)** 'In showing the weaknesses of the disciples Mark was letting the early Church down.' Do you agree? Give reasons for your answer, showing you have considered more than one point of view. (5)

**2** 'Go into all the world and preach the good news to all creation.' Give two examples of ways in which the Church today carries out Jesus' instructions. (8)

Now try these questions with no hints. Before you write an answer try to write down your own hints on how to score full marks.

**3** **(a)** Describe the call of the first four disciples. (6)

**(b)** Why did Jesus decide to have a group of disciples with him? (4)

**4** 'For Christians to live up to Jesus' teaching on discipleship, they must be part of a Church community. They cannot go it alone.' Do you agree? Give reasons for your answer, showing you have considered more than one point of view. (5)

## How to score full marks

**1** **(a)** This is a question to test what you know. Make sure you give a full account. The marking will be on a point-by-point basis; not every detail will be required for full marks, but every significant point would have to be made.

**(b)** This is an evaluation question, testing your ability to give opinions. Make sure you cover more than one point of view.

**2** This question tests knowledge and understanding. Note the eight marks; the answers need to be quite full.

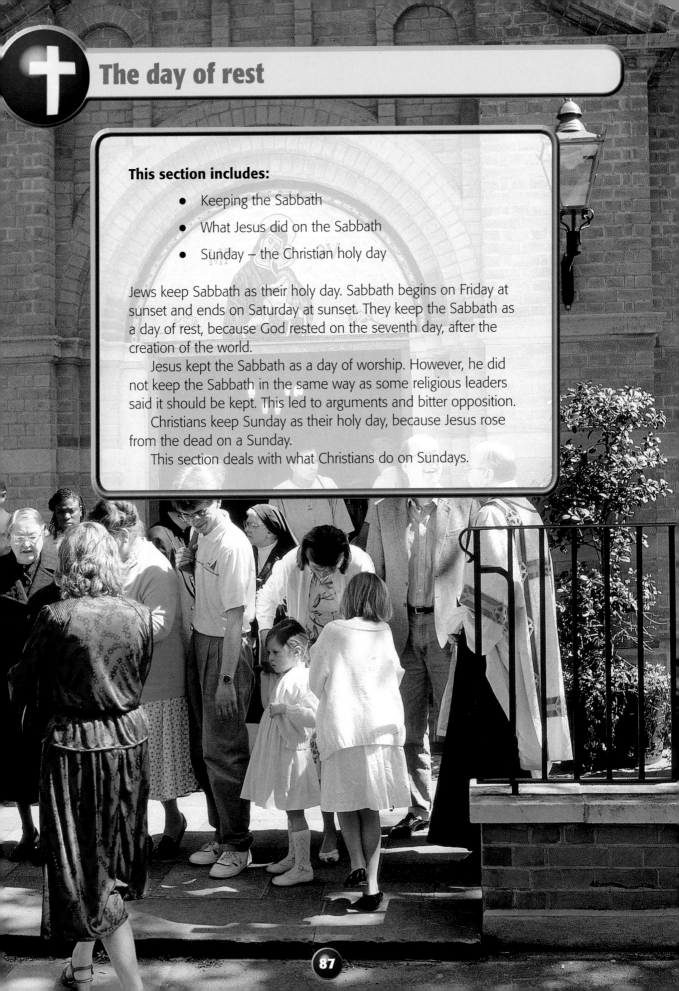

# The day of rest

**This section includes:**

- Keeping the Sabbath
- What Jesus did on the Sabbath
- Sunday – the Christian holy day

Jews keep Sabbath as their holy day. Sabbath begins on Friday at sunset and ends on Saturday at sunset. They keep the Sabbath as a day of rest, because God rested on the seventh day, after the creation of the world.

Jesus kept the Sabbath as a day of worship. However, he did not keep the Sabbath in the same way as some religious leaders said it should be kept. This led to arguments and bitter opposition.

Christians keep Sunday as their holy day, because Jesus rose from the dead on a Sunday.

This section deals with what Christians do on Sundays.

## The Sabbath

The Sabbath is the holy day of the Jews. It falls on a Saturday, the seventh day of the week.

The word Sabbath means rest. The Sabbath is a day of rest. According to Genesis chapters 1 and 2, the Sabbath is the day on which God rested after creating the world.

> By the seventh day God had finished the work he had been doing; so on the seventh day he rested from all his work. And God blessed the seventh day and made it holy, because on it he rested from all the work of creating that he had done. (Genesis 2: 2-3)

## The way Jews observe the Sabbath

### The Fourth Commandment

One of the Ten Commandments states that the Sabbath should be observed every week. It makes two basic statements about the Sabbath.

- The Sabbath is holy. It is a day set apart for God.
- The Sabbath is a day of rest.

> Remember the Sabbath day by keeping it holy. Six days you shall labour and do all your work, but the seventh day is a Sabbath to the LORD your God. On it you shall not do any work, neither you, nor your son or daughter, nor your manservant or maidservant, nor your animals, nor the alien within your gates. For in six days the LORD made the heavens and the earth, the sea, and all that is in them, but he rested on the seventh day. Therefore the LORD blessed the Sabbath day and made it holy. (Exodus 20: 8-11)

For Jews the Sabbath is a day to treasure. It is a family occasion. Since the Sabbath runs from sunset on Friday to sunset on Saturday, all the family gather to share the Sabbath meal on the Friday evening. Saturday is the day for going to the synagogue.

*The woman of the household welcomes in the Sabbath.*

The Sabbath is also a day of rest. Unnecessary work should be avoided.

The Sabbath rules were observed in the time of Jesus. Naturally people wanted to know just what 'you shall not do any work' meant – what you could do and what was forbidden. One document containing teachings of the Rabbis lists 39 activities which were not allowed on the Sabbath, including sowing, ploughing, reaping, baking, weaving and lighting a fire. People obviously asked for detailed rules and some of those rules dealt with very small matters. If a stove was already warm cooked food could be put on it. If a kettle in which there was hot water was taken off a stove, the hot water could be used, but cold water could not be put into the kettle so that it could boil.

## Jesus in the synagogue

Jesus went to the synagogue on the Sabbath. It was a custom for anyone who had anything to say to the people present in the synagogue to be invited to speak.

> They went to Capernaum, and when the Sabbath came, Jesus went into the synagogue and began to teach. The people were amazed at his teaching, because he taught them as one who had authority, not as the teachers of the law.

Just then a man in their synagogue who was possessed by an evil spirit cried out, 'What do you want with us, Jesus of Nazareth? Have you come to destroy us? I know who you are – the Holy One of God!'

'Be quiet!' said Jesus sternly. 'Come out of him!'

The evil spirit shook the man violently and came out of him with a shriek.

The people were all so amazed that they asked each other, 'What is this? A new teaching – and with authority! He even gives orders to evil spirits and they obey him.' News about him spread quickly over the whole region of Galilee. (Mark 1: 21-8)

- Jesus had no formal training such as was given to the teachers of the law, who might normally be expected to speak in the synagogue. Such teachers would pass on to others what they had been taught about the scriptures and the way in which the scriptures should be interpreted and obeyed.

- People were amazed because Jesus spoke with authority. He was not passing on what he had learned from other teachers. His teaching was original, new and powerful. He spoke with personal authority.

- The man with an evil spirit was suffering from some psychological illness. He spoke as though it was the evil spirit speaking. He announced that Jesus was the Holy One of God. What people would make of that title we can only guess. Remember, this event took place at the very beginning of Jesus' ministry. Hardly anyone would have even heard of him, in all probability.

- Jesus spoke to the evil spirit, not to the man. Whether Jesus believed that there really was an evil spirit in the man, or whether he simply accepted what the man himself believed, we cannot be sure. What Mark's Gospel makes clear is that Jesus spoke and the man was cured.

- Those around were even more amazed. What sort of authority was this? To teach with authority, as Jesus did, was impressive enough. To be able to give orders to evil spirits and have those orders obeyed was even more remarkable.

No wonder that news of what Jesus had said and done spread very quickly throughout the district.

- Jesus had healed the man on the Sabbath. No one seems to have criticized Jesus because he had done this on the Sabbath.

- Naturally many people wanted to bring their own family members and friends to be healed by Jesus. They brought them as soon as they could – when the Sabbath was over! They waited till after sunset rather than bring sick people to Jesus on the day of rest.

That evening after sunset the people brought to Jesus all the sick and demon-possessed. The whole town gathered at the door, and Jesus healed many who had various diseases. He also drove out many demons, but he would not let the demons speak because they knew who he was. (1: 32-4)

## Activities

1 Hot seat: The teacher (or, better, a member of the Jewish community) talks about the Jewish Sabbath. **C 2.1a**

2 Do you think it is important for a family regularly to sit down for a meal together? Give reasons for your answer. **PS 2.1**

## Key points

- One of the Ten Commandments states that the seventh day is to be kept as a holy day, a day of rest, because God created the world in six days and rested on the seventh day.

- Jews keep Saturday as the Sabbath, the day of rest. Some teachers laid down very precise rules as to what one could or could not do.

- Jesus preached in the synagogue and healed a man on the Sabbath day. Everyone was amazed by his authority.

# What Jesus did on the Sabbath

## People start to find fault with Jesus

When Jesus healed the man with an evil spirit in the synagogue at Capernaum, everyone was amazed. There were no protests about him having broken the Sabbath law. However, a little later in his ministry some religious leaders began to resent what Jesus was saying and doing. You can see the way this opposition builds up in a series of incidents in chapters 2 and 3 of Mark's Gospel.

- A paralyzed man was brought to Jesus to be healed. Some people standing nearby were upset when Jesus told him his sins were forgiven. They didn't say anything, but Jesus knew what they were thinking and said so (2: 1-12, see page 16).

- Jesus visited Levi the tax-collector and had a meal at his house. This time the Pharisees did speak – but to the disciples, not Jesus. Jesus heard them and answered that he had come for sinners, not righteous people (2: 13-17).

- This time people came to Jesus to criticize his disciples for not fasting. The disciples of John the Baptist and the Pharisees did fast. Note that the criticism was only that they did not follow a tradition. They had not broken the Law (2: 18-22).

So, Jesus' critics were looking for a chance to catch him out. Their chance came over the law of the Sabbath.

### On the Sabbath – in the cornfields

On the first occasion it was the disciples who were accused of breaking the Sabbath law.

> One Sabbath Jesus was going through the cornfields, and as his disciples walked along, they began to pick some ears of corn. The Pharisees said to him, 'Look, why are they doing what is unlawful on the Sabbath?'

> He answered, 'Have you never read what David did when he and his companions were hungry and in need? In the days of Abiathar the high priest, he entered the house of God and ate the consecrated bread, which is lawful only for priests to eat. And he also gave some to his companions.'

> Then he said to them, 'The Sabbath was made for man, not man for the Sabbath. So the Son of Man is Lord even of the Sabbath.' (2: 23-8)

- The disciples were simply picking ears of corn and, apparently, eating them. According to the law, they were allowed to do so. The law said, 'If you enter your neighbour's cornfield, you may pick the ears with your hands, but you must not put a sickle to his standing corn.' However, reaping was one of the things forbidden on the Sabbath – and that was what the disciples were accused of doing.

- Jesus didn't argue about what the disciples were doing. He was more concerned about the basic idea behind the Law. The Law was there for the good of the human race, not to make life difficult and complicated. The consecrated bread in the shrine was for the priests to eat. That was the law; it meant that the priests had a legal right to that food. But when David and his men were hungry and the priests offered them some of the bread, of course it was all right for them to accept.

- Jesus had shown the Pharisees that the law was for the benefit of the human race. That applied to the Sabbath law as well. 'The Sabbath was made for man, not man for the Sabbath.'

- Then Jesus made a comment which showed that he realized what the Pharisees were getting at. They were challenging his authority. Very well – 'The Son of Man is Lord even of the Sabbath' (see the unit on Son of Man, pages 16–17).

## On the Sabbath – the man with the shrivelled hand

The next incident described was a put-up job. People were in the synagogue waiting to see if Jesus would heal a man with a shrivelled hand. There was no urgency about the man's case. His hand could just as well have been healed the next day, when the Sabbath was over. What would Jesus do?

> Another time he went into the synagogue, and a man with a shrivelled hand was there. Some of them were looking for a reason to accuse Jesus, so they watched him closely to see if he would heal him on the Sabbath. Jesus said to the man with the shrivelled hand, 'Stand up in front of everyone.'
>
> Then Jesus asked them, 'Which is lawful on the Sabbath: to do good or to do evil, to save life or to kill?' But they remained silent.
>
> He looked around at them in anger and, deeply distressed at their stubborn hearts, said to the man, 'Stretch out your hand.' He stretched it out, and his hand was completely restored. Then the Pharisees went out and began to plot with the Herodians how they might kill Jesus. (3: 1-6)

- Jesus realized right away what was happening. He didn't avoid the situation. He faced his critics openly.

- Note how Jesus worded his question. 'Which is lawful on the Sabbath…' In other words, what is the Sabbath law about? Is the Sabbath about rules and regulations? Or is it about doing good?

- His opponents said nothing. Jesus was angry because of their attitude. He healed the man.

- The Pharisees plotted against Jesus. They went to the Herodians, who were presumably the supporters of King Herod. Jesus was seen as a threat to the political authorities as well as to the religious leaders.

### Activities

1. Make a list of things which must be done, even on a day of rest. **PS 2.1**

2. Christians think of Jesus as the example of a perfect human life. Yet in the incident involving the man with a shrivelled hand Jesus is said to have been angry. Is it ever right to be angry? Give reasons for your answer, showing you have thought about more than one point of view. **PS 2.1**

### Key points

- Jesus said that the Law of God was given for the benefit of the human race. It was not meant to be full of petty rules and restrictions.

- Jesus showed by what he said and what he did that it was right to do good on the Sabbath. The law was not intended to make life difficult on the Sabbath.

# Sunday – the Christian holy day

## Why Sunday?

Two points you must remember when writing about the Christian observance of Sunday:

- Christians keep Sunday, the first day of the week, as their holy day. The Christian Sunday is not the same as the Jewish Sabbath, which is on a Saturday.

- The reason Christians keep Sunday as their holy day is that it is the day on which Jesus rose from the dead.

  When the Sabbath was over, Mary Magdalene, Mary the mother of James, and Salome bought spices so that they might go to **anoint** Jesus' body. Very early on the first day of the week, just after sunrise, they were on their way to the tomb. (16: 1-2)

**Be sure to note:**
- Christians do NOT keep Sunday as their holy day because God rested on the seventh day after he had created the world. That is the reason why Jews observe Saturday as the Sabbath. Some Christians see Sunday as the Christian Sabbath – but that is not the reason for Christians choosing Sunday.

- Christians do not keep Sunday as their holy day because the Holy Spirit came to the apostles on a Sunday. Christians do celebrate Pentecost or Whitsun as the day of the coming of the Spirit and it always falls on a Sunday – but that is not the reason for Sunday being the Christian holy day.

- Do not be confused by the fact that some people talk about Monday as the beginning of the week. Christians do not count Sunday as the seventh day.

## What does Sunday mean to Christians?

For Christians, Sunday is a day of worship. Many Christians make it a rule to attend church every Sunday, or on most Sundays, if they are able to do so.

It is a Christian duty to worship God. An important part of worship is regular private prayer and Bible reading. Meeting together with other Christians is also important.

- Christians meet to praise God together. They receive support and encouragement from each other as they worship.

- Jesus told his disciples to take bread and wine. As he gave them the bread, he said, 'This is my body'. As he gave them the wine he said, 'This is my blood'. Most Christians believe they must obey Jesus' command to receive the bread and wine in remembrance of him, as he told them.

- The Bible is precious to Christians. They learn of the Bible by hearing it read aloud and by hearing sermons which explain the relevance of the Bible today. Others meet for Bible study in groups.

Christians can worship in all these ways at any time. Since Sunday is their holy day, they are more likely to worship on this day.

Note that you may get a question such as 'Do you think people can be called proper Christians if they do not worship in church even though they are able to do so?' You will receive no marks if you answer 'They may be too ill to go to church or they may have to work on Sundays'. The words in the question '… even though they are able to do so' should tell you not to write about people who are not able to go to church.

## Is Sunday a Christian version of the Jewish Sabbath?

Many Christians understand Sunday as a day of rest. They take the fourth commandment as applying to the way Christians should observe Sunday. The commandment says that the day should be holy, set aside for God. Also, it is God's will that one day each week should be, for most people, a day of rest.

These Christians are reasonable about their beliefs. They accept that many people must work to meet the needs of modern society. They limit the work they do on a Sunday to the bare minimum. They are against the opening of shops and other activities which seem to make Sunday just like any other day. Some Christians, such as nurses and ambulance drivers, may have to work on Sundays and so not be able to go to church.

Many people, not only Christians, like Sunday to be a day with a different character. They believe that it is good for society as a whole that there should be a day which is quieter and with fewer pressures. They feel it is important that there can be a day when a family can expect to be together. If Sunday is a normal working day then many parents will have to work and will not be able to spend the day with their children.

## What about people who are not Christians?

Although shops are allowed to open for a number of hours on Sundays, there are still restrictions laid down by the law of the land which say what people can do. These restrictions are designed to respect Christian attitudes to the keeping of Sunday. The restrictions apply to everyone, Christian or otherwise. It might seem unfair that people who do not believe in the Christian faith have to keep laws which make people keep Sunday as a holy day.

Jonathan Edwards, winner of the gold medal for the triple jump in the 2000 Olympic Games, found it difficult to come to terms with competing on a Sunday because of his Christian beliefs.

### Activities

1   Visit the website of the Lord's Day Observance Society (www.lordsday.co.uk). What are the basic principles of the society? How far do you agree with those principles? **IT 2.1, 2.2**

2   Imagine that, to allow better use of facilities at your school, Year 7 came to school from Monday to Friday, Year 8 from Tuesday to Saturday, Year 9 from Wednesday to Sunday, Year 10 from Thursday to Monday and Year 11 from Saturday to Wednesday. Would it matter? Give reasons for your answers, showing you have thought about more than one point of view. **PS 2.1**

### Key points

- For Christians, Sunday is a day for worship.
- Many Christians see Sunday as being the Christian equivalent of the Jewish Sabbath.

# Exam questions to practise

Below are some sample exam questions about the day of rest. The first two have examiner's tips to give you some hints on how to score full marks. The others are for you to try on your own. A good idea is to work out your own hints on how to score full marks before answering them.

**1** **(a)** Describe what happened when Jesus and his disciples walked through a cornfield on the Sabbath. (6)

   **(b)** Why did their actions make the Pharisees so angry? (4)

**2** 'You can be a Christian without going to church.' Do you agree? Give reasons for your answer, showing you have considered more than one point of view. (5)

Now try these questions with no hints. Before you write an answer try to write down your own hints on how to score full marks.

**3** Choose and describe a miracle Jesus performed on the Sabbath. Why did the onlookers react as they did? (8)

**4** **(a)** Why is Sunday the Christian holy day? (1)

   **(b)** What might a Christian mean by 'holy' when talking of Sunday as a holy day? (3)

## How to score full marks

**1** **(a)** A question to test your knowledge. Note the six marks – you must cover all that is done and said.

**(b)** This question is testing your knowledge and understanding. If you are in doubt, read the chapter again.

**2** An evaluation question. As always, answer fully, considering as many different viewpoints as you can

# The Eucharist

**This section includes:**

- The origins of the Eucharist
- The significance of the Eucharist
- Celebrating the Eucharist – I
- Celebrating the Eucharist – II

At the Last Supper Jesus took bread and wine and gave it to the disciples. He told them that the bread and the wine were his body and blood. He said 'Do this in memory of me'.

Almost all Christian traditions have Communion services at which the bread and wine are taken in memory of Jesus. Christians understand the Eucharist in different ways.

The section includes the rites of five denominations.

# The origin of the Eucharist

## The Last Supper

To many Christians the Eucharist is the central ceremony of their worshipping life. It is a memorial of Jesus' last meal before he died. By sharing in a simple meal of bread and wine, Christians remember the saving power of Jesus' death and resurrection as members of the family of the Church.

Jesus shared a meal with his disciples on the evening before he died. Christians call this meal 'the **Last Supper**'. It took place in an upstairs room in a house in Jerusalem.

On the first day of the Feast of Unleavened Bread, when it was customary to sacrifice the Passover lamb, Jesus' disciples asked him, 'Where do you want us to go and make preparations for you to eat the Passover?'

So he sent two of his disciples, telling them, 'Go into the city, and a man carrying a jar of water will meet you. Follow him. Say to the owner of the house he enters, 'The Teacher asks: Where is my guest room, where I may eat the Passover with my disciples?' He will show you a large upper room, furnished and ready. Make preparations for us there'.

The disciples left, went into the city and found things just as Jesus had told them. So they prepared the Passover.

When evening came, Jesus arrived with the Twelve. While they were reclining at the table eating, he said, 'I tell you the truth, one of you will betray me – one who is eating with me'. They were saddened, and one by one they said to him, 'Surely not I?' 'It is one of the Twelve', he replied, 'one who dips bread into the bowl with me. The Son of Man will go just as it is written about him. But woe to that man who betrays the Son of Man! It would be better for him if he had not been born'.

While they were eating, Jesus took bread, gave thanks and broke it, and gave it to his disciples, saying, 'Take it; this is my body'. Then he took the cup, gave thanks and offered it to them, and they all drank from it. 'This is my blood of the new covenant, which is poured out for many', he said to them. 'I tell you the truth, I will not drink again of the fruit of the vine until that day when I drink it anew in the kingdom of God'. (14: 12-25)

## The preparations for the Passover meal

Two disciples are sent into Jerusalem with precise instructions to look for a man carrying a jar of water. This would have been a most unusual sight as the collecting of water was considered to be a woman's duty. Jesus may have made an arrangement previously with the man so that the disciples could be quietly guided to a suitable room for their Passover celebrations.

## The prediction of Judas' betrayal of Jesus

While the Passover meal was being eaten, Jesus warned the disciples that one of them would betray him. The disciple is not mentioned by name, and the revelation obviously came as a shock to the others. Was Jesus trying to warn Judas of the seriousness of the action he was about to take?

## Jesus' words over the bread and wine

Having given thanks to God, Jesus broke the bread and offered it to the disciples. 'This is my body', he said. Jesus' actions and words symbolize the fact that his body would be broken on the cross. Taking a cup of wine he said, 'This is my blood of the new covenant, which is poured out for many'. The wine is another symbol of Jesus' approaching death. But his death will not be meaningless; it will bring about a new and lasting covenant between God and his people.

'I will not drink again of the fruit of the vine until that day when I drink it anew in the kingdom of God'

Jesus understood that this was to be his last meal. However, his words may have a deeper meaning. The Jews believed that, at the end of time, there would be a Messianic banquet when the faithful would celebrate with God in his kingdom. Jesus' work was now finished, but he would celebrate with his followers again in the kingdom of God.

## The Passover

Jesus' Last Supper with his disciples was a Passover meal. For the Jews, Passover remembers the time early in their history when God, through Moses, saved the Jewish nation from slavery in Egypt.

The Old Testament book of Exodus describes how God sent a series of plagues on the land of Egypt to persuade Pharaoh to let the Jewish slaves go free. Nine plagues came and went, but Pharaoh refused to release the Jews. Then, following instructions from God, Moses told each Jewish household to kill a lamb and smear its blood on their door posts. The lamb was to be roasted and eaten. During the night, an angel came to each home in Egypt. The firstborn son in every Egyptian family died; but the angel *passed over* the Jewish houses because of the blood on the doorposts. The Jews were set free that night.

Since that time, Jews have looked upon this event as the time when their covenant relationship with God began, sealed with the blood of the sacrificial lambs.

### Links between Passover and the Eucharist

God rescued the Jews from slavery in Egypt.

*The Jewish festival of Passover celebrates the time when God saved the Jews from slavery in Egypt. It is also a reminder of their covenant relationship with God.*

*Sharing the bread and wine of the Eucharist unites the family of the Christian Church.*

Christians believe that God rescued all people from sin through Jesus Christ. His death and resurrection brought about a new covenant between God and the human race, sealed with the blood of Christ.

Christians look upon Jesus as the Lamb of God, who sacrificed himself for the sins of the world. Sharing the bread and wine of the Eucharist is the way in which Christians remember Christ's saving death and resurrection, and celebrate being members together of the world-wide Church.

### Activities

1   In many cultures sharing a meal is a sign of fellowship. Why do you think this is the case? **PS 2.1**

2   Hot seat: Student as one of the disciples talking about the Last Supper. **C 2.1a , 2.1b**

### Key points

- The Eucharist is a sacred meal at which Christians remember the Last Supper Jesus shared with his disciples.

- Christians believe that Jesus' words over the bread and wine symbolize the fact that his sacrificial death would bring about a new covenant between God and the human race.

# The significance of the Eucharist

## Why celebrate the Eucharist?

Christians have always met to celebrate the Last Supper Jesus ate with his disciples. For many, it is the main act of worship. In 1 Corinthians 11: 23-5 Paul tells the people of Corinth that its authority comes from Jesus Christ:

> The Lord Jesus, on the night he was betrayed, took bread, and when he had given thanks, he broke it and said, 'This is my body, which is for you; do this in remembrance of me'. In the same way, after supper he took the cup, saying, 'This cup is the new covenant in my blood; do this, whenever you drink it, in remembrance of me'.

Most Christians share bread and wine together because Jesus asked his followers to do so in memory of him. However, the names by which the service is called, the understanding of the meaning of Jesus' words, and the frequency with which it is celebrated varies from tradition to tradition.

## Titles given to the Eucharist

*Eucharist* This is a Greek word meaning 'Thanksgiving'. By sharing the bread and wine, Christians give thanks for the death and resurrection of Jesus, and for the covenant relationship with God which has been made possible by Jesus' sacrifice. The title is used in a number of traditions.

*Holy Communion* The word '**communion**' means to take part in something as a group or family. Christians meet together as a family to share the bread and wine. This title is popular among Anglicans and the Free Churches.

*Mass* The title **mass** is used by Roman Catholics and some Anglicans. The service was once read in Latin, and the final sentence was 'Ite, missa est', which means 'Go, you are sent on a mission'.

At the end of the service, the congregation are sent out to continue their Christian mission, having been strengthened by the fellowship of the Church and the sacrificial body and blood of Jesus.

*Liturgy* In this sense, the word 'Liturgy' means to give an offering or a service. Christians who use this title, among them the Orthodox, look upon the ceremony as an opportunity to offer praise to God and to give their lives to his service.

Note that the word Liturgy is also used to describe parts of the rite – e.g., Liturgy of the Word, Liturgy of the Sacrament. The word is used in this way in the next two units.

*Breaking of Bread* This title reminds Christians of the origin of the service. Jesus broke bread and shared it among his disciples at the Last Supper. Today, Christians share in this simple meal in memory of Jesus' death and resurrection.

*Lord's Supper* In the same way as the disciples shared Jesus' last supper, Christian disciples today can share in the same meal in the spiritual presence of Jesus. Some Baptist Churches use this name.

## How often do Christians celebrate it?

Anglican, Roman Catholic and Orthodox Christians regard the Eucharist as their principal act of worship. The Eucharist is celebrated every Sunday, and often during the week as well.

Baptist, Methodist, United Reformed and other Free Churches may celebrate the Eucharist once or twice a month. Their worship is pulpit-centred and, therefore, the main emphasis of each service is on readings from the Bible and preaching.

The Salvation Army and the Society of Friends (the Quakers) do not have Eucharistic services. These Christians do not believe that outward symbols are important. They believe that the most important part of Christian worship is to accept Jesus Christ into their hearts. They honour Christ's sacrifice on the cross in the way they live their lives.

## The bread and wine of the Eucharist

From the time of the first followers of Jesus Christians have believed that, at the Eucharist, they have received the Body and Blood of Christ. This belief is based on the words that Jesus used at the Last Supper:

> This is my body ... This is my blood of the covenant which is poured out for many.

Because of this, the bread and wine used at the Eucharist are special.

For some Christians the bread and wine have special significance because in some sense they become the body and blood of the risen Christ.

Such language can be very puzzling, even for Christians. Throughout the history of Christianity, and in all the different Church traditions, attempts have been made to explain exactly what happens (if anything) to the bread and wine when they are blessed or consecrated. There have been fierce arguments, and complicated words (such as transubstantiation and consubstantiation) have been invented as people tried to explain it. Today there is general agreement that just how the bread and wine of the Eucharist become the body and blood of Christ is essentially a mystery. A mystery can be believed, even though it cannot be explained!

Other traditions understand the Eucharist to be a family meal. Jesus told his followers to eat and drink bread and wine in his memory. They believe very strongly that Jesus is present among them when they meet. But they do not believe that he is specially present in the bread and wine nor that the elements of the meal become his body and blood.

Some Christian traditions feel it is important to use unleavened bread (bread without yeast to make it rise), often in the form of specially made individual wafers. Jesus would have eaten unleavened bread (bread without yeast) at the Last Supper as it took place at Passover, when Jews eat this type of bread in memory of the Israelite exodus from Egypt. By eating unleavened wafers, Christians are following the example of Jesus. Others are quite content to use ordinary bread and emphasize the significance of sharing a single loaf.

*Prayer over the bread and wine.*

Many traditions use ordinary wine for the Eucharist, while others use non-alcoholic wine or some other fruit-based substitute. Most Churches use a single cup (chalice) for distributing the wine, others use small individual glasses.

## Points of agreement

Most Christians would agree that:

- at the Last Supper Jesus asked his followers to share bread and wine in his memory and therefore instituted the Christian Eucharist
- at the Eucharist Christians thank and praise God for the death and resurrection of Jesus
- Jesus is present among Christians at the Eucharist in a real and special way
- Christians share a fellowship meal with each other and the risen Christ.

### Activities

1 'How the bread and wine of the Eucharist become the body and blood of Christ is essentially a mystery. A mystery can be believed, even though it cannot be explained.' Is it reasonable to believe in something even if you do not understand it? **PS 2.1**

2 An example of something people believe in but do not necessarily understand is electricity. Is that the same sort of mystery? **PS 2.1**

### Key points

- The Eucharist was instituted by Jesus at the Last Supper.
- Christians believe that the risen Christ is present among the community as they share a fellowship meal with each other.
- Many Christians believe that the risen Lord is present in the bread and the wine, which become his body and blood.
- The Salvation Army and the Quakers do not celebrate the Eucharist.

## Anglican Rite

This is how Anglicans celebrate the Eucharist.

### Introductory rites

- After a hymn and an introductory prayer the people ask God's forgiveness for what they have done wrong. The Ten Commandments or the Two Great Commandments may be read.

- The Gloria, a hymn of praise, is either said or sung by everyone. The hymn includes these words: 'Lord God, heavenly King, almighty God and Father, we worship you, we give you thanks, we praise you for your glory.'

### Liturgy of the Word

- There are either two or three readings from the Bible. The last reading is always from one of the gospels and, in fact, is called the Gospel.

- The priest preaches the sermon, based on the Bible readings or on any special theme for the day.

- The people join in the words of the Creed.

- Then follows the Intercession, a time of prayer for the Church, the world, the local community, those who suffer or who are ill, and those who have died.

### Liturgy of the Eucharist

- In many churches the priest and the congregation offer each other the sign of peace.

- The bread and wine and the offerings of the congregation are brought to the altar in a procession. The priest offers the gifts to God. The congregation join in the offering by saying, 'All things come from you, and of your own do we give you.'

- The priest says the Eucharistic prayer. He says over the bread and wine, 'grant that by the power of your Holy Spirit these gifts of bread and wine may be to us his body and his blood.'

- He says the words of Jesus at the Last Supper, ending with the words 'Do this in memory of me'.

- The congregation says together the words of the Lord's Prayer.

- Before receiving the bread and wine, they ask for God's forgiveness – 'Lamb of God, you take away the sins of the world, have mercy on us…'.

- The congregation receives communion. Unleavened wafers are used. The priest says to each communicant, 'The body of Christ' and 'The blood of Christ'. In the Anglican Church, children usually first receive communion at the age of eleven, if they have been confirmed.

- Afterwards there is a short time of silent prayer. The priest blesses the people and says, 'Go in peace to love and serve the Lord.' The congregation reply, 'Thanks be to God.'

## Roman Catholic

### Introductory rites

- All the people make the sign of the cross, and the priest greets everyone. There is a hymn and a prayer.

- The priest invites the people to reflect on what they have done wrong, and to ask for God's forgiveness. He leads the people in the Kyrie, 'Lord, have mercy, Christ have mercy, Lord have mercy'.

- The Gloria, a hymn of praise, is either said or sung by everyone. The hymn includes these words: 'Lord God, heavenly King, almighty God and Father, we worship you, we give you thanks, we praise you for your glory.'

### Liturgy of the Word

There are usually three readings from the Bible. Between each reading a few verses from a psalm are said or sung.

- The first reading is from the Old Testament, the second from the New Testament (often from one of the letters of St Paul), and then there is a procession in which the Bible is carried to the lectern. A passage from one of the Gospels is read by the priest.

- The priest will give a homily, or sermon. It is usually based on the Bible readings.
- The people join together in the words of the Creed.
- Then follows the Prayer of the Faithful, in which the congregation pray for God's blessing on those present at the Eucharist, on those who suffer, and on those in need of God's mercy.

## Liturgy of the Eucharist

- The bread and wine and the offerings of the congregation are brought to the altar in a procession. The priest offers the gifts to God. He says, 'Lord God, we ask you to receive us and be pleased with the sacrifice we offer you with humble and contrite hearts.'
- The priest washes his hands and says the Eucharistic Prayer. He says over the bread and wine, 'Let them become for us the body and blood of Jesus Christ.'

*Some churches use unleavened communion wafers …*

*… others use ordinary bread.*

*The Exchange of the Peace is a feature of both Anglican and Roman Catholic Eucharists. People greet each other with the words 'Peace be with you'.*

- He says the words of Jesus at the Last Supper, ending with the words 'Do this in memory of me.'
- The congregation says together the words of the Lord's Prayer.
- The priest and the congregation exchange the peace.
- Before receiving the bread and wine, the people ask for God's forgiveness – 'Lamb of God, you take away the sins of the world, have mercy on us…'.
- The congregation receives communion. Unleavened wafers are used. The priest says to each communicant, 'The body of Christ' and 'The blood of Christ'. In the Roman Catholic Church, children can receive communion from the age of seven as part of their preparation for confirmation.
- Afterwards there is a short time of silent prayer. The priest blesses the people and says, 'Go in peace to love and serve the Lord'. The congregation reply, 'Thanks be to God'.

### Activities

1 Watch a video of a Eucharist in either of these traditions. How does it fit the pattern given here? **PS 2.1**

2 Some people find the exchange of the Peace very significant and meaningful. Why is this the case? **PS 2.1**

### Key points

- In both the Anglican and Roman Catholic traditions, the person leading the service is a priest. He or she is called the celebrant.
- People who receive communion in these traditions (communicants) have usually been baptized and confirmed, though Roman Catholic children often receive their first communion some years before they are confirmed.

## Greek Orthodox (The Liturgy)

Greek Orthodox Churches call the Eucharist 'The Liturgy'. This is how they celebrate it.

### Liturgy of the Word

- The congregation sings hymns and prays. There is a reading from the Bible. It may be taken from the Acts of the Apostles or one of the letters.

- The priest carries the book of the Gospels from behind the **iconostasis** towards the people. This is called the Lesser Entrance. The priest sings the Gospel passage.

- A sermon may follow at this point. Sometimes it is given at the end of the service.

### Liturgy of the Faithful

- The communion gifts of bread and wine are taken in a procession through the congregation. They are carried through the Royal Doors of the iconostasis and placed on the altar. This is known as the Greater Entrance. The bread would have been baked at home by a member of the congregation.

- Prayers are said for the leaders of the Church, for the world and for the local community. Everyone sings the words of the Creed and the Lord's Prayer.

- The Royal Doors are closed. At the altar, behind the doors, the priest thanks God for sending his Son to save the world. He recites the words of Jesus at the Last Supper.

- The bread is divided into four parts. One part is put whole into the chalice with the wine; the second part is divided among the clergy serving at the Liturgy; the third part is cut into small pieces and placed in the chalice for the communion of the people. These three sections of bread and the wine are consecrated, or blessed, by the priest to be the body and blood of Jesus. The fourth part is also cut into small pieces and placed on a dish. This section of the bread is not consecrated.

- The priest invites the congregation to approach the iconostasis for communion with the words, 'In fear of God, in faith and love, draw near.' In the Greek Orthodox Church, babies and small children may receive the bread and wine as soon as they have become members of the Church through baptism and chrismation (see page 110).

- The bread and wine are given together on a spoon to each person by name. A small tray is held under the chin to catch any spillage. The mouth is wiped with a cloth. The communicant will then kiss the chalice.

- Once the congregation has received communion, prayers of thanksgiving are said. At the end of the service, the priest stands in front of the Royal Doors with the pieces of unconsecrated bread. As each member of the congregation takes a piece of the bread they will either kiss a small cross held by the priest or they will kiss the priest's hand.

*An Orthodox service is divided into two parts by the iconostasis, a screen decorated with icons. The Royal Doors in the iconostasis are opened to allow the priest to bring the consecrated bread and wine to the people. This symbolizes the breaking down of the barrier of sin between God and mankind through the death of Jesus.*

## Methodist

The Methodist order of service is similar to that used in the United Reformed Church. Methodists call the Eucharist 'Holy Communion' and normally celebrate it once or twice a month, on 'Sacrament Sunday'. It usually takes place after the main service.

- The minister says the Prayer of Thanksgiving over the bread and wine. This tells the story of the Last Supper and is taken from one of the Gospels (for example, Mark 14: 22-5) – 'This is my body. This is my blood.'

- The people are invited to the communion table: 'Receive the body of Christ which was given for you and the blood of Christ which was shed for you, and feed on him in your hearts by faith and thanksgiving.' Ordinary bread and either grape juice or unfermented wine are used. Individual cups are sometimes used rather than a chalice from which all receive the wine.

- After the communion there is a prayer of thanksgiving. The people are sent out into the community with the words, 'Go in peace in the power of the Spirit to live and work to God's praise and glory.'

## Baptist

The communion service in this tradition is more informal and is often referred to as the Lord's Supper. Baptist Churches do not use a set order of service and the pattern of the service will vary from Church to Church. However, the essential elements will be the same. The Lord's Supper is usually held once or twice a month.

- The minister opens the service by inviting the people to follow the command of Jesus at the Last Supper to take bread and wine 'in memory of me'. The invitation is open to all who 'Truly and earnestly repent of their sins and are in love and fellowship with their neighbours'.

- The minister will read the account of the Last Supper over the bread and wine. This may be taken from 1 Corinthians 11: 23-6. The congregation is reminded that Jesus asked his followers to take bread and wine in remembrance of him. The bread and wine are seen as symbols of his body and blood –

'This is my body, which is for you. This cup is God's new covenant, sealed with my blood.' A deacon or elder of the church says a prayer of thanksgiving for Jesus' sacrifice on the cross.

- The people remain in their seats as the bread is taken to them by the deacons or elders. The bread used is ordinary bread. Each person takes a piece, eats it and prays in silence. Wine or grape juice is distributed in small individual cups. The congregation wait until everyone has been served and then drink together as they would at a family meal.

- The service ends with a prayer of thanksgiving. A hymn or chorus may be sung.

*Receiving communion in the Methodist tradition.*

### Activities

1 Listen to some music used at a traditional Orthodox Liturgy. In what way would such music contribute to the atmosphere during the service? **PS 2.1**

2 Why is it important to Baptists that communion is open to all who 'are in love and fellowship with their neighbours'. **PS 2.1**

### Key points

- In these, as in many traditions, the reading of Scripture and prayer for anyone in need are essential parts of the Eucharist.

- Although communion in some traditions is less frequent, the Last Supper is no less valued.

# Exam questions to practise

Below are some sample exam questions on the Eucharist. The first two have examiner's tips to give you some hints on how to score full marks. The others are for you to try on your own. A good idea is to work out your own hints on how to score full marks before answering them.

1  Describe a service of the Eucharist in a tradition of your choice. (8)

2  **(a)** Name two Christian traditions which do not celebrate the Eucharist. (2)
   **(b)** Why do they think it unnecessary to do so? (3)

Now try these questions with no hints. Before you write an answer try to write down your own hints on how to score full marks.

3  Describe what Jesus said and did when he took bread and wine at the Last Supper. (4)

4  In what ways is the Bible used in a Eucharist? (4)

## How to score full marks

1  It is important, first, to say which tradition you have chosen and, second, to make sure you are writing about the tradition you have chosen. Your marks will drop sharply if you fail on either of these points. Note the eight marks. You need to describe the whole service, not just the part surrounding the act of communion.

2  This question is a straightforward test of your knowledge and understanding.

# Baptism

**This section includes:**

- Baptism in Mark's Gospel
- Infant baptism
- Infant baptism services
- Believers' baptism
- A believer's baptism service

This section looks at baptism, which has been the Christian initiation ceremony from the time of Jesus himself. Some Christians believe that infants should be baptized and welcomed into God's family. Other Christians believe that only those who are old enough to make a true commitment to Jesus as Saviour should be baptized.

Both groups believe in baptism with water in the name of the Father, the Son and the Holy Spirit.

The section includes the reasons for both infant and believers' baptism and an account of the rites.

Baptism is an initiation ceremony. This is a ceremony that makes a person a member of something. In this case, someone who is baptized becomes a member of the Christian community.

A number of Christian traditions teach that Baptism is a **sacrament**, which means that it is an outward sign of the giving of God's grace and salvation to a person. Christians look upon baptism as the beginning of a life-long relationship with God.

## How did baptism begin?

Baptism has been an important part of Christianity since the earliest days of the Church. It has its roots in the Jewish religion. Ritual washing was a Jewish ceremony, and the Jewish Law gave instructions for bathing in running water. Jews would enter this water to make themselves ritually clean. This ceremony would be performed every time a Jew wanted to be cleansed before taking part in a religious service or activity.

There are a number of occasions in the New Testament which show the importance of baptism for the early Christians.

- Mark's Gospel begins with John the Baptist. He was preaching in the desert and he had an urgent message: turn away from your sins and *be baptized*, and God will forgive your sins (1: 4).

Mark records that many people came to John in the desert to repent of their sins and to be baptized. John's baptism was to prepare people for the coming of the Messiah. It was a public sign that they had turned away from their old selfish lives, and were making a new start. The waters of baptism washed away their sins.

- Jesus, himself, was baptized by John in the River Jordan.

  As Jesus was coming up out of the water, he saw heaven being torn open and the Spirit descending on him like a dove. And a voice came from heaven: 'You are my Son, whom I love; with you I am well pleased.' (1: 9-11)

Jesus' ministry was about to begin. Christians look upon the baptism of Jesus as an act of dedication to God and to the task ahead of him. It was a new beginning. Also, by being baptized, Jesus showed his approval of baptism.

*Jesus was baptized at the beginning of his work for God.*

- At the end of Mark's Gospel, Jesus gives his final instructions to the disciples:

  Go into all the world and preach the good news to all creation. Whoever believes and is baptized will be saved. (16: 15-16)

From the earliest days of Christianity, baptism was seen as an important act of commitment and salvation. Those who came to believe in Jesus were to be baptized and, in doing so, they would be saved, rescued from their sins.

On the Day of Pentecost, a few weeks after the ascension of Jesus into heaven, Peter spoke to a large crowd who had come to Jerusalem for the Jewish festival. He told them of Jesus, of his death and resurrection. He also appealed to them to turn away from their sins and be baptized. Many were baptized that day (Acts 2: 14-42).

There is a clear pattern running through stories of baptism in the early Church. One experience naturally leads to another:

- belief in Christ as the Son of God

- repentance of sins and God's forgiveness
- baptism
- the giving of the Holy Spirit (see below).

Baptism became an outward, visible declaration of belief, repentance, and dedication to God and his Son, Jesus. Unlike the cleansing rituals of the Jewish faith, Christian baptism was only to be performed once, and this has continued to the present day.

At first, those who were baptized were adults. Later, Christians wished their children to be baptized so that they too could join the family of the Church.

## Baptism today

Most Christian traditions encourage baptism. It is seen as important because:

- it allows a person to make a fresh start
- sins are washed away
- it enables a Christian to share in the death and resurrection of Jesus
- it invites God into a person's life
- it gives strength to resist temptation
- it unites a Christian with other Christian worshippers.

Many Christians believe that the gift of the Holy Spirit is given at baptism. The Holy Spirit enters the baptized person and gives new life; their life is dedicated to God. The ceremony marks a new beginning in the Christian's life. It is a fresh start.

Christians believe that a person who has been baptized has been born again. Christians also say that when a person receives the Holy Spirit it brings them closer to Jesus, and gives them the strength to become more like him. Through water and the Holy Spirit, baptism is a symbol of new life and salvation.

Note that Christians do not believe that the Holy Spirit can only be received through baptism. The Spirit moves freely and can come to anyone at any time.

Water is used in all Christian baptisms. Water is symbolic of two beliefs:

1 As water is essential for life, so baptism brings spiritual, eternal life.

2 As water is used to cleanse, so baptism brings inner cleanliness. The soul is cleansed of sin.

*The dove is one of the Christian symbols for the Holy Spirit.*

The Salvation Army and the Society of Friends (the Quakers) do not hold services of baptism because they think it is unnecessary to have outward, visible symbols of their commitment. It is not the ceremony that is important, but the personal and close relationship each believer has with God.

There are two methods by which Christians are baptized today:

- pouring water on the head (see page 110).
- total immersion (see pages 110, 112–14).

In both types a commitment is made to turn away from evil and to love God. They are baptized in the name of the Father, Son and Holy Spirit. This commitment is made either by the individual or, in the case of the infants, by their representatives.

### Activities

1  Are initiation ceremonies important? Give reasons for your answer. **PS 2.1**

2  Many religions use water in their rites. Why do you think this is so? **PS 2.1**

### Key points

- Jesus himself was baptized.
- The apostles baptized those who joined the Church, as Jesus had told them to do.
- Baptism enables a Christian to share in Jesus' death as they do in his resurrection.
- Christians are baptized with water in the name of the Father, Son and Holy Spirit.

## Baptizing children

Those who turned to Christianity in the early days of the Church wished their children to be baptized as well. As baptism symbolizes the beginning of new life, it seemed right that children should be welcomed into the family of the Church at an early age. They could then grow up surrounded by the beliefs and teachings of the Church.

Today, infant baptism is the most common Christian initiation ceremony. A large number of traditions baptize young children, including:

- Anglican
- Methodist
- Orthodox
- Roman Catholic
- United Reformed Church.

The method of baptism is usually by the sprinkling of water on the head. However, in the Orthodox Church, young children are fully immersed in the water.

It is important to remember that these traditions also baptize older children and adults who were not baptized as infants. In this case, the person being baptized makes a conscious decision to be initiated into the Church. Before the baptism there is usually a period of instruction in the beliefs of Christianity and in the meaning of the ceremony. During the baptism service water is poured on the head as it is in infant baptism but, here, the person is old enough to make their own promises.

## Why is infant baptism thought to be important?

There are three main answers to this question.

1 *To cleanse the child of original sin.*
   It is difficult to imagine an infant being capable of sin. At such a young age they do not know the difference between right and wrong. However, many Christians believe that all people are born with the ability to sin, to go against the wishes of God.

   Sin is anything which makes people not good enough to be in the presence of God.

The human nature children inherit from their parents has a weakness which makes people likely to sin. This weakness is called **original sin**.

The water of baptism is seen as a sign of the Holy Spirit entering the life of the child, giving it the strength to fight these basic instincts as it grows up. Through baptism original sin is taken away.

2 *To bring the child into the family of God.*
   Many Christian parents want their children to become members of their church's congregation from an early age. During the baptism service, the parents and godparents promise to provide a Christian upbringing for the child, and to encourage the child to make its own commitment to God at a **confirmation** ceremony when older. The whole congregation welcomes the child and promises to support the parents in bringing the child up as a Christian.

3 *To bring the love of God to a sick child.*
   If a child is born weak and is struggling to live, Christian parents may request that the child is baptized at the hospital. Should the child live, a ceremony should be held at a church later so that the child can be welcomed into the family of God by the congregation.

*A font is used in infant baptism. In many traditional churches, the font is positioned near to the door to symbolize the belief that a person enters the family of God through the waters of baptism.*

As part of the Church of Christ, we all have a duty to support *them* by prayer, example and teaching. As *their* parents and godparents, you have the prime responsibility for guiding and helping *them* in their early years. This is a demanding task for which you will need the help and grace of God.

(From the Common Worship baptism service)

## What is the role of parents and godparents?

If the person to be baptized is an infant, then the statements of belief and promises to God cannot be made by the child. Parents are the most important influence on a child's life. They are the ones who are responsible for making sure that the child is brought up in a Christian environment. At infant baptism, parents declare their own faith and promise to pass on that faith to their child.

To help them with this duty, godparents will be chosen by the parents before the ceremony. The godparents agree to share the responsibility of educating the child in the Christian faith. Together, parents and godparents make a commitment during the ceremony to:

- provide the child with a Christian environment in which to grow up
- pass on the teachings of the Church
- encourage the child to attend Church regularly
- teach the child about God and how to worship him
- teach the child how to pray
- encourage the child to be confirmed at a later date.

Examination candidates often make the mistake of saying that godparents promise to look after the child in the event of the parents' death. This is *not* the case, as you can see from the list.

*The candle given at baptism symbolizes Jesus, the light of the world, coming into the life of the person baptized. Some people light the candle each year on the anniversary of the baptism.*

### Activities

1 Make a list of the criteria which should guide parents in the choice of godparents for their children. **PS 2.1**

2 When you have finished your list, check it against the list of the duties of parents and godparents above. **PS 2.3**

### Key points

- The majority of Christians practise infant baptism.
- Through infant baptism a child is freed from original sin and made a member of the Church, the family of God.
- A commitment is made by the parents and godparents that the child will be given a Christian upbringing and eventually brought for confirmation.

# Infant baptism services

This unit looks at infant baptism services in three traditions.

## Anglican baptism

Baptisms often take place during a Eucharist or family service. This enables the members of the church to welcome the child. It can also take place more privately, with only family and a few friends present.

The main points of the service are:

- the parents and godparents agree to help the child to grow up as a Christian. They promise to pray for the child and to set a good example of Christian living
- the priest makes the sign of the cross on the child's forehead
- the priest may invite the parents and godparents to sign the child with the cross
- the child's family gathers with the priest at the font and the water of baptism is blessed
- the congregation joins with the parents and godparents in stating their belief in God as Father, Son and Holy Spirit
- the child is baptized with water being poured on the head three times, and with the words, '(Name), I baptize you
        in the name of the Father,
        and of the Son,
        and of the Holy Spirit. Amen.'
- the parents and child may be given a lighted candle. This represents the light of Christ in the child's life
- the congregation welcomes the child into the family of God.

## Orthodox Baptism

- The godparents answer for the child when they are asked to renounce evil and turn to Christ. They also read the Creed on behalf of the child.

- The water in the font is blessed and prayers are said for the child.
- The child is anointed with oil.
- The child is immersed three times in the water and baptized 'in the name of the Father, and of the Son, and of the Holy Spirit.'
- The child is dried with a towel and dressed in a baptismal robe.
- A cross is put around the neck of the child. This is a sign that the child has taken up the cross of Christ.
- The baptism is immediately followed by a service of **chrismation**, or confirmation. This represents the seal of the Holy Spirit on the life of the child. **Chrism**, or holy oil, is placed on the child's head, eyes, lips, ears, chest, hands and feet.
- After chrismation, the child is carried three times round the font.
- At the end of the service, a small lock of hair is cut as a sign of dedication to God.

'Bradley, I baptize you in the name of the Father, and of the Son, and of the Holy Spirit. Amen.'

# Roman Catholic Baptism

In this tradition, baptism usually takes place during a service of Holy Communion.

- The child, parents and godparents are welcomed by the priest at the entrance of the church. They are asked why they have brought the child to the church.

- The sign of the cross is made on the child's forehead by the priest, parents and godparents.

- Bible readings are followed by a homily from the priest, during which the meaning of baptism is explained.

- The child is anointed with oil. This is a sign that the child is dedicated to God.

- The parents and godparents say that they reject Satan. They say the words of the Creed on the child's behalf.

- The child is immersed or water is poured on the head three times. While this is being done, the priest will say, 'I baptize you in the name of the Father, the Son and the Holy Spirit'.

- The child is anointed with chrism and clothed in a white baptismal robe.

- A candle is lit from the **paschal candle** and given to the child's parent. This is a sign that the light of Christ will guide the child through life.

*The paschal candle, renewed every Easter, is a symbol of the resurrection. The candle given at a baptism is lit from the paschal candle to show that baptism represents dying to sin and rising with Christ to new life.*

## Activities

1 Make enquiries about local churches of different traditions which practise infant baptism. Whereabouts in the building is the font? Is there any significance in its position? **PS 2.1**

2 Are there any members of the class who have recently attended an infant baptism? If so, they should give a short talk about what happened. **C 2.1b**

## Key points

In all three traditions, there are four important elements in infant baptism:

- water

- the words of baptism – 'I baptize you in the name of the Father, and of the Son and of the Holy Spirit. Amen.'

- the promises and statements of belief made by the parents and godparents on behalf of the child. In the case of an older child or adult being baptized, they will make the promises and statements themselves.

- the acceptance of the child into the family of God.

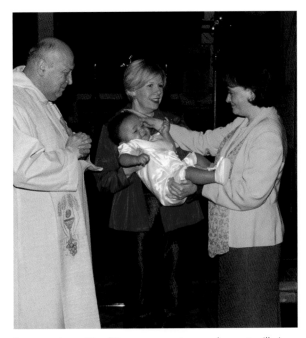

*In a number of traditions, a parent or godparent will sign the child with the cross.*

# Believers' baptism

Believers' baptism is practised by the following traditions:

- Baptist Churches
- Pentecostal Churches
- other Evangelical traditions.

It is the baptism of those who are old enough to make their own decision. The candidate understands the commitment being made. The method of baptism is by **total immersion**. The ceremony may take place in a pool inside the church building. A candidate may also be baptized in a river, swimming pool, the sea, or other source of running water.

## Why is it thought to be important?

- In the days of the early Church, adults who came to believe in Jesus Christ as Saviour and Lord were baptized. Those who follow the practice of believers' baptism say that Jesus was baptized as an adult. They wish to follow his example.
- The word 'baptize' comes from the Greek term 'baptizo', meaning 'to dip'. Many people believe that total immersion follows the way in which the first Christians were baptized.

At the beginning of Mark's Gospel, John the Baptist is introduced as one who was preaching to all who came to him in the desert. The Messiah was coming. John's task was to prepare people for the arrival of God's Son. His message was clear:

> Turn away from your sins and be baptized, and God will forgive your sins. (1: 4)

Those who came to believe in Jesus requested baptism as a public sign of:

- their belief
- their repentance of sin and a desire to begin a new way of life
- their wish to follow the teachings and commandments of Jesus.

These ideas were echoed by Peter in his speech on the day of Pentecost. He said this to all those who were interested in the Christian faith:

> Repent and be baptized, every one of you, in the name of Jesus Christ for the forgiveness of your sins. And you will receive the gift of the Holy Spirit. (Acts 2: 38)

Today, believers' baptism follows this practice. Belief in Christ comes before baptism. Baptism is seen as important for the following reasons:

- baptism is an outward sign of belief in Christ and the teachings of the Church
- the candidate has chosen to be a Christian. Love of Jesus leads to a commitment to dedicate the person's life to Christ.

## What is its meaning?

Many Baptist churches, and some other traditions, have a small pool, or **baptistry**, for the baptism of adults. It is situated at the front of the building to show the importance of baptism. The design of the pool reflects the symbolism Baptists see in baptism.

*A baptistry.*

At believers' baptism, Christians wish to identify themselves with the death and resurrection of Jesus.

There is usually a period of instruction before the baptism takes place. Once a person requests baptism, the minister of the church may speak to the Christian over a number of weeks to make sure that the request is genuine and that the person is fully aware of the commitment they are making. The candidate will be taught the meaning of baptism and their responsibility as a full member of the church.

To be born again is important for those who practise believers' baptism. However, it should be noted that being born again is not part of the process of baptism for these Christians. They do not request baptism because they wish to be born again; they wish to be baptized because they have been born again.

The service of believers' baptism is an outward sign and declaration of the changes that have taken place in the person's life through belief in Jesus. Following baptism, the Christian is expected to play his or her part in spreading the Christian message, avoiding sin, and loving all people as children of God.

# A believer's baptism service

## *An outline of the service*

Traditions which practise believers' baptism do not use a set form of service. Therefore a service of baptism will vary a little from church to church. A service will contain the following points.

- The minister gives a sermon to explain the importance of baptism. It is the outward sign of inner renewal by the Holy Spirit. He may call upon the congregation to remember their own baptism, and to renew their commitment to Jesus.

- Those who wish to be baptized are called forward. There are usually a number of candidates, and each one is called forward in turn. They often wear light or white clothing. This symbolizes forgiveness and new life.

- The candidates are asked if they have repented of their sins and if they have faith in the Lord Jesus Christ.

- Each candidate may read a short passage from the Bible which is important to them. They may also give a testimony, explaining how they came to be Christians and why they wish to be baptized. Alternatively they may state their faith by answering a series of questions.

- The candidate enters the pool by a set of steps. This shows that they wish to leave their old, sinful life behind.

- The candidate and minister step into the pool. The minister will say, '(Name), because you have repented of your sins and have requested baptism, I now baptize you in the name of the Father, and of the Son and of the Holy Spirit. Amen.'

- The candidate is gently and briefly immersed in the water. This is a sign that the old way of life has died, and that the Christian is buried in the same way as Jesus was buried for three days in the tomb.

- The candidate leaves the pool. This symbolizes that the Christian's new life has begun. Jesus rose from the dead, and the candidate has risen to new life with Christ.

- As the candidate comes out of the water the congregation may sing a hymn chosen by the candidate. The minister may give the newly baptized person a few quiet words of encouragement. A friend, or sponsor, will be waiting at the top of the steps with a towel. This person will have been chosen by the candidate as someone who has been important and supportive in his or her spiritual life. The candidate is led off to change and will then return to the service.

An experience of believers' baptism.

*Why did you want to be baptized?*
I believe that the Bible teaches that once a person has invited Christ into his or her life, the next stage is to be baptized. This is an outward sign to family and friends of the difference God has made in the person's life. I knew that my baptism would please God, and I welcomed the chance to invite my non-Christian friends and family to my baptism.

*Was there a period of preparation?*
Once I had decided to be baptized, I was taken through a period of preparation. The meaning of baptism was explained to me by the elders of my church. They wanted to make sure that I was requesting baptism for the right reasons.

*What was your testimony?*
During the service of baptism, I gave a testimony to the congregation. My conversion to Christianity was not particularly dramatic. It was more of a gradual process. For my testimony, I chose to openly pray for God's protection over my life, to thank him for being with me to that point, and to ask him to help me move forward.

*How did you feel during the service?*
The baptism service was very moving and a highlight of my life. My friends and family were very supportive, and I felt God's presence as the other three candidates and I were baptized. I really believe that it was God's strength that brought me to that point and supported me through the service.

*Has baptism made a difference to your life?*
Since my baptism, I feel more confident in my faith. Everyone who knows me understands that I am living for Christ and that my inspiration comes from him. I feel that I am more respected in my church community; everyone knows what I believe. I am now in a position to move forward for God and to tell those I meet of God's love.

(Jennifer Smith, aged 16, from Liverpool)

## Activities

1   There are *three* common features present in the baptism ceremonies of all traditions. Identify these features from the illustration. What is the significance of each feature? **PS 2.1**

2   Visit a church with a baptistry and talk to the minister and others there about the way they understand what baptism is about. Make notes on what you have been told. **PS 2.1**

## Key points

- Believers' baptism is normally by total immersion.
- Those who are baptized have already made the decision to become Christians.
- At baptism they witness publicly to their commitment to Christ.
- Going into and out of the water symbolizes dying to sin and rising to new life.

# Exam questions to practise

Below are some sample exam questions on baptism. The first two have examiner's tips to give you some hints on how to score full marks. The others are for you to try on your own. A good idea is to work out your own hints on how to score full marks before answering them.

1   Look at the picture on p. 113
    (a) Explain what is happening. (2)
    (b) What commitment will the person being baptized have made? (4)
    (c) Give two reasons why some Christians believe people should be baptized in this way. (4)

2   Describe an infant baptism in any Christian tradition. You must name the tradition you have chosen; it need not be one of the three described on pages 110–11. (6)

Now try these questions with no hints. Before you write an answer try to write down your own hints on how to score full marks.

3   Why do some Christians believe it is right to baptize infants? (6)

4   Do you think a member of the Salvation Army could accept an invitation to be a child's godparent? Give reasons for your answer, showing you have considered more than one point of view. (5)

## How to score full marks

1   This is a question to test what you know. It will be marked on a point by point basis. In both (b) and (c) there are some detailed points to be made which will, if clearly made, receive two marks rather than one.

2   Note that while the question says 'any Christian tradition', you cannot choose one which does not baptize infants! This answer will need continuous writing and will be marked by levels of response.

## Coursework is an essential part of the GCSE examination

You will have to produce one piece of coursework of 1000–1500 words on Mark's Gospel. 20% of the total mark for the course is awarded for coursework.

In your coursework you will be assessed on:

- what you know about Mark's Gospel and how it has influenced what people believe and do (Knowledge)

- your ability to explain what Christians believe and how their beliefs affect the way they live and worship (Understanding)

- your ability to give a personal opinion, while showing you appreciate other points of view (Evaluation).

**You will be marked separately on these three objectives.**
**It is important that all three skills are shown.**

### *Knowledge*

It is not enough merely to gather as much information as you can! You need to show that you know what is really important. Look at this example.

> ### Task
>
> Select one person from Mark's Gospel who was called to discipleship, describing clearly the call, the person's response and the challenges s/he experienced.

### Answer

The rich man (10: 17-22)
A very rich man went up to Jesus. The man wanted to know what he had to do to receive eternal life. Jesus told him to obey the commandments and the man said he has always done this. Jesus then told him to sell all his possessions, give the money to the poor, and follow him. When Jesus said this he was challenging the man to give away something that meant a great deal to him. But the man could not bear to give up material possessions, even for eternal life. He turned and walked away. Even then, he was sad because he realized what he was turning down.

### Comment

This is a good choice. There is enough in the Gospel for the candidate to write about the call, the response and the challenge. All the main points are concisely and clearly made.

The candidate has not simply told the story but has picked out the most important things.

This part of the assignment is testing knowledge – the ability to select the right material and to present it accurately. Even so, she has shown understanding as well – and would receive credit for doing so. For instance, the last sentence about the man turning away sadly showing understanding about just what the challenge was and how the man responded to it.

So, make careful choices.

- When you have a choice of subject, make sure you choose someone or something about which there is enough to say.

- Read the question carefully. What is it about the person/thing that answers the question? Make sure that everything relevant is there. At the same time, leave out anything that is not asked for.

- Do not merely copy out the story. If you do, you will not be showing that you can select the right material properly.

### *Understanding*

You have shown what you know. Now you need to show that you understand.

In fact, you have shown some understanding already. You show understanding by the way you select and comment on material. Now you must go further to show that you are aware of the significance of the information you have given.

Make sure you know what the question is really asking. Look at this example.

## Task

In what ways can Jesus' commission to the disciples be carried out in the twenty-first century?

## Answer

In Mark 16: 15-18, Jesus told his disciples that they must preach the gospel, baptize believers, drive out evil spirits and heal the sick. Modern Christian disciples can carry out Jesus' instruction in different ways. Some become priests, ministers or missionaries; they preach the gospel and they baptize those who are to join the Church. Others spread the gospel by talking about their faith to people they meet in their daily lives. Others feel that they can spread the news of God's love by caring for people who are ill. Many doctors and nurses see their work as a vocation. Some Christians believe they must oppose what is obviously evil, wrong or unfair. A union official would think it a Christian duty to defend a worker who was being unfairly treated.

## Comment

This candidate has said clearly what the commission is. The examples show her understanding. Each example relates to one part or other of the commission. She has taken a first century idea (driving out evil spirits) and given a valid twenty-first century parallel (injustice). Correct terms, such as priest, missionaries and vocation, have been used.

There are many more examples which could be given but, since there is a word limit, the moderator would expect no more than what is given here.

So, show that you understand:
- what the key words are and what they mean
- what the religious importance is
- what religious people would feel.

## Evaluation

You have shown what you know and understand. Now you need to say what you think. You must show that you understand more than one point of view. You need not make a final judgement; you can simply give two or more points of view and say what you think is good or bad about each.

## Task

'It is better to be baptized when you are older'. Do you agree?

## Answer

I think that people should be baptized when they are old enough to know what they are doing. They have come to know Jesus in a personal way and want to commit their lives to him. The decision to be baptized is theirs. Believers' baptism means exactly what it says – it is the baptism of believers; unlike infant baptism, in which promises are made on behalf of the baby by parents and godparents. Believers' baptism is a way of showing others your love of God and that you want to follow a Christian way of life. Also, in Mark 1: 9-11, we are told that Jesus was baptized when he was an adult. So I think that must be the best example to follow.

But some Christians think that you should be baptized as a baby. This is because the child will become a member of the family of the Church at an early age. The child will grow up learning to love God with the help of the people in the church and the godparents. Some Christians think that as we are humans we are born into a sinful world and baptism cleans us from these sins. I also think that parents of sick babies find real comfort in knowing that their child has been baptized.

## Comment

This is a balanced answer. The candidate has given his own point of view based on good knowledge and understanding. It is quite a strong argument and the points are clearly made. He then gives another point of view in a fair and balanced way. It may not be his opinion, but his approach is positive – he does not criticize the beliefs of others. It is important to give more than one point of view. Full marks will not be given for answers that have only one point of view, however good the answer is.

You will notice that when the stronger candidates quote from the Bible they give the reference (book, chapter, verses). You should always do the same when writing your assignments. See the section Gathering Information on the next page.

# Writing your assignment

Before you start to write your assignment make sure you understand what you have to do. Read the title a number of times and try to see what the assignment is really about.

## Gathering information

1   Books will probably be your main source of information.

   - Make sure you can understand the books you use, otherwise what you write may be very muddled.

   - What you take from the books must be relevant to the topic.

   - Do not copy everything from the book word for word. You must show that you can understand what you are writing. Use your own words.

   - You can use short quotations when there is a good reason to do so – such as quoting a person's exact words or a passage from scripture. If you do, put the quotation in inverted commas and give the exact reference.

   - If you use a book, make a note of the title, author and publisher. You will need to list your sources on the Coursework Cover Sheet.

2   You may wish to make use of the Internet.

   - You will not receive any credit just because you have found something on the Internet! You will receive credit if you make good use of what you have found.

   - You must realize that, while some books are written as resource material for people doing coursework and other research, websites are not.

   - Much of what has been said about the use of books applies also to websites.

   - If you use a website, make a note of the name and address. You will need to list it among your sources on the Coursework Cover Sheet.

3   Interviews are an important way of getting information and opinions.

   - Be sure in your mind why you want to talk to this person and what you need to learn from the interview. Remember that the person to whom you are talking may not understand what you need to know.

   - Prepare carefully for the interview. Read about the subject first. Have a list of questions ready.

   - Take a tape recorder (and spare tapes) with you, to record the conversation – if the person you are interviewing agrees.

   - Don't forget evaluation. Ask questions about the person's opinions.

4   The subject of your assignment may be suitable for a survey.

   - Make sure you understand what the survey is for. Do you wish to find out what people know or what they think? If you ask people 'What is a miracle?' you are asking what they know. If you ask people, 'Do you believe miracles can happen today?' you are asking what they think. Your survey can, of course, include both sorts of question.

   - Make sure you interview a reasonable number of people. If you ask too few, your survey will be too limited. If you ask too many, you will have too much information to include. 20–25 is a good number. Even so, make clear that you understand that this is a small sample. Among a sample of 20 people a majority may think that God does not answer prayer. A sample of 200 or 2000 may think otherwise.

   - Try to ask people of different ages, backgrounds and gender. Remembering that this is a Religious Studies assignment, try to have people of different denominations. Also, try to get a mixture of people who are very committed to their faith, people who are not so committed and those who have no faith at all.

- Word the questions carefully. Give people a chance to say what they really think. For example, imagine you are writing an assignment on the day of rest. You might include the question 'Do you think shops should open on Sundays?' Many people will simply answer 'Yes' or 'No'. Some may want to answer, 'It depends on the circumstances.' If you ask the question, 'Can you think of circumstances in which Christians would approve of shops opening on Sundays?' you are giving people a chance to say what they really think. Listen to their answers and write them down carefully.

- Once you have completed your survey, try to analyze the information and the opinions you have been given. For example, do young people's views differ from older people's? Do the views of males differ from the views of females? If there are differences, why do you think they are there?

- If you can, use a diagram, chart or graph to show what the figures mean.

5   What you can find out for yourself is important. If there is something local to do with your assignment, go and look for yourself. Take some photographs. Note carefully what you see and hear. Check if you need permission first.

## After gathering your information

- Before you start writing, read the assignment title again. If you are not sure about anything in the title, or what you have to do, ask your teacher to explain.

- Have you enough information to answer *all* parts of the question? Check each part to make sure.

- Make sure that everything you are going to use is relevant to the question. If it isn't relevant, don't use it – however interesting it may be. Such material will gain you no marks.

## Preparing to write

Remember to ask yourself again – 'What will the moderator give me marks for?'

- You must remember that you are writing about one particular faith – Christianity, based on the story of Jesus in Mark's Gospel.

- You need to show that you understand what is important in that particular faith.

- What do these people believe? How does what they believe affect what they do? What are their attitudes to the big moral issues?

- In some parts of the assignment you will be asked what you think. Make sure that you show that you understand both sides of the argument – you will get more marks for this than for just giving your own point of view. Even then your own opinion is important.

## Writing your assignment

- It is a good idea to begin each part of your assignment on a separate piece of paper. If you do, you can work on the different sections in any order you like. If you make any mistakes, you may not have to rewrite quite as much.

- Marks are given for spelling, punctuation and grammar. Be careful to avoid mistakes.

- You must use your own words! Do not copy long passages straight from a book. A good idea is to read the passage, close the book, then write out what you want to say in your own words. Open the book again and check that what you have written is accurate.

- Use correct religious terms. It is better to say Jesus taught in parables rather than in stories.

## Using illustrations

It is usually a good idea to use illustrations – as long as they are relevant to the assignment and you explain how they are relevant to the assignment.

## When you have finished

- Your teacher will give you a Coursework Cover Sheet. Fill it in carefully. You may want to practice with a photocopy.

- At the end of the assignment you should make a list of the books you have used. If you have had any help from someone other than your teacher, say so.

- Read the assignment carefully. Check that you have answered all parts of the question.

**Abba** Aramaic word children used when speaking to their fathers. It means, literally, 'Dad' or 'Daddy'

**Adoration** Loving and worshipping God

**Angel** A spiritual being, believed to act as a messenger of God

**Anglican** A member of any Church which belongs to the Anglican Communion

**Anglican Communion** A world-wide fellowship of Churches, including the Church of England and the Church of Wales

**Anoint** To smear or dab with oil, usually as part of a religious ceremony

**Apostle** One who is sent out on a mission

**Aramaic** The language spoken in Palestine at the time of Jesus. Mark gives the actual Aramaic words in three places in the gospel (5: 41; 7: 34; 15: 34)

**Ascension** The word used to describe how Jesus left earth to return to the Father in heaven

**Baptism** To dip in or pour on water as a sign of admission into the Christian community

**Baptistry** A pool used for believers' baptism

**Blasphemy** Using the name of God insultingly or wrongly

**Celebrant** Title given to the priest who leads the celebration of the Eucharist

**Charisma** Great attraction or charm that can inspire devotion in others

**Chrism** A sweet-smelling oil used in baptism

**Chrismation** A ceremony of anointing with oil (chrism) immediately following baptism in the Orthodox Church

**Christ** The Greek name for the promised leader sent by God

**Church** When spelled with a capital 'C', Church means Christian people; when spelled with a small 'c', a building, a Christian place of worship

**Commission** The order given by Jesus after the resurrection that his disciples were to go and preach the gospel to the whole world

**Communion** Christian fellowship; the taking of the bread and wine in Christian fellowship

**Confession** An admission of having done something of which one is ashamed, accompanied by repentance and a wish to be forgiven

**Confirmation** A ceremony at which Christians who have been baptized make public their own promises of faithfulness to God. If they were baptized as infants they accept the promises made at their baptism by their parents and godparents. They receive the gift of the Holy Spirit

**Conservatives** People who believe the Bible is inspired but is not a scientific text

**Consubstantiation** The belief that at the Eucharist the bread and wine become the body and blood of Christ while in no way ceasing to be bread and wine

**Covenant** A sacred, binding agreement between God and human beings

**Convent** A religious community of women; a house for a group of nuns

**Creed** A statement of beliefs

**Crucifixion** Death caused by being fixed to a cross

**Day of Atonement** The most solemn day of the Jewish year. A day to ask forgiveness of God for sins committed

**Disciple** One who wishes to follow and learn from another; in the New Testament, used of the followers of Jesus, especially the Twelve

**Eternal life** Everlasting life with God

**Eucharist** The ceremony at which Christians celebrate what Jesus said and did at the Last Supper

**Exorcism** The act of driving away evil spirits

**Faith** Belief and trust which is so complete that it involves following the person in whom you place your trust

**Fundamentalists** People who believe that the Bible is completely inspired by God, and cannot contain errors.

**Glory** The quality which humans can sense that sets God apart from and above them

**Gospel** Literally means 'good news'; the four books in the Bible describing the life of Jesus are called the four Gospels

**Herodians** Supporters of the Jewish royal family and of the Roman occupation

**Holy of Holies** The holiest part of the temple, where God was thought to be more present than anywhere else

**Holy Spirit** The third person of the Trinity. Christians believe the Holy Spirit is always with them, giving them strength and support

**Hosanna** A Hebrew word meaning 'save now', often used as a shout of greeting and honour

**Iconostasis** A screen in an Orthodox church separating the congregation from the altar and covered with icons of Jesus, Mary and the saints

**Intercession** To ask something for someone else, usually in prayer

**Kingdom of God** Where God's greatness and authority are accepted. Jesus taught that it exists not only in heaven but also in the hearts of his followers

**Laity** Christians who are not ordained as priests or ministers

**Last Supper** The meal which Jesus shared with his disciples on the night before he was crucified

**Liberals** People who believe that the writers of the Bible, though guided by God, were human and made mistakes

**Literalists** Fundamentalists who believe in the exact literal interpretation of scripture

**Mass** Name given to the Eucharist by Roman Catholics and some Anglicans

**Messiah** Hebrew name for the promised leader sent by God (Christ is the same word in Greek)

**Messianic secret** On a number of occasions Jesus stressed that his disciples were not to tell people that he was the Messiah. Until people realized the sort of Messiah Jesus was, he did not want them to think of him as Messiah at all

**Miracle** A wonderful, supernatural act beyond the power of the human race

**Mission** Going out, or being sent out with a special purpose; for Christians that purpose is to spread the gospel

**Missionary** Someone who takes the teachings of their religion to other people, usually to other countries

**Nun** A woman who has dedicated her life to God, usually living with other nuns in a convent community

**Oral tradition** Stories passed on by word of mouth

**Original sin** The idea that all people are born with a tendency to sin

**Parable** A story told by Jesus to illustrate his teaching

**Paschal candle** A large candle which burns at all services between Easter and Ascension. The five wounds of the crucified Jesus are marked on the candle. At a baptism, a candle is lit from the Paschal candle as a symbol of the light of Christ

**Passover** Jewish festival celebrating the Exodus, the escape from Egypt

**Patriarch** Father and head of a family or tribe. In the Old Testament book of Genesis, Abraham, Isaac and Jacob are called patriarchs

**Persecuted** To be attacked and suffer for one's beliefs

**Petition** To ask something for oneself, usually in prayer

**Pharisees** A party of religious lawyers at the time of Jesus, devoted to keeping the Law of Moses. They created many interpretations of the Law for the Jews to follow

**Prayer** Communicating with God

**Preparation Day** The day before the Sabbath

**Prophecy** A message from God, very often foretelling the future

**Prophet** Someone who speaks the will of God, a messenger

**Rabbi** A Jewish teacher, leader of a Jewish community

**Repent** To be sorry for your actions or sins; to turn away from sin and make a fresh start

**Resurrection** A restoration of life after death; usually refers to Jesus' returning to life after his death on the cross

**Rite** A form of service

**Ritual** A solemn religious ceremony, which is repeated regularly

**Sabbath** The Jewish holy day; it begins at sunset on Friday and ends at sunset on Saturday

**Sacrament** A rite or ritual (e.g., baptism) through which the worshipper receives a special gift of grace, a spiritual gift from God

**Sacrifice** An offering to God

**Sadducees** A party of Jewish priests at the time of Jesus. They controlled the worship in the temple in Jerusalem

**Salvation** To be saved from sin. Christians believe that the death and resurrection of Jesus saved humanity from sin, and made possible a new and close relationship with God

**Sanhedrin** The supreme court of Jewish Law in Israel

**Saviour** Christians believe in Jesus as the person who, through his death and resurrection, has saved his followers from their sins

**Scribes** Experts on Jewish Law. Also, those who made copies of the Jewish Scriptures

**Son of David** A title for the Messiah, who would be descended from King David and would, like him, be a great leader

**Son of God** A title given to Jesus emphasizing that he always existed, in the presence of the father, before his birth at Bethlehem

**Son of Man** A heavenly being with special authority from God

**Synagogue** The main place of Jewish meeting and worship other than the Temple. There was a synagogue in every Jewish village or town

**Testimony** At a believers' baptism, the candidate may speak of how they came to believe in Jesus Christ and the important role he plays in the life of the Christian

**Torah** The Jewish Law/the Hebrew Bible

**Total immersion** A form of baptism which involves being completely submerged under water

**Transfiguration** The occasion when Jesus was seen in glory with Moses and Elijah

**Transubstantiation** The belief that at the Eucharist, when the bread and wine become the body and blood of Christ, there is a change in the substance (real nature) of the bread and wine

**Trinity** Christians think of God as three Persons but only one God; the Persons are the Father, the Son and the Holy Spirit

**Vocation** A sense of being called to perform a task for God

**Zealots** A party of patriotic Jews who were violently opposed to the Roman occupation of Israel. They were prepared to use force to regain their country's freedom

# Index